# Libraries Supporting Online Learning

# Libraries Supporting Online Learning

## Practical Strategies and Best Practices

Christina D. Mune

An Imprint of ABC-CLIO, LLC

Santa Barbara, California • Denver, Colorado

**Library of Congress Cataloging-in-Publication Data**

Names: Mune, Christina D., author.
Title: Libraries supporting online learning : practical strategies and best practices / Christina D. Mune.
Description: Santa Barbara, California : Libraries Unlimited, [2020] | Includes bibliographical references and index.
Identifiers: LCCN 2020029647 (print) | LCCN 2020029648 (ebook) | ISBN 9781440861758 (paperback ; acid-free paper) | ISBN 9781440861765 (ebook)
Subjects: LCSH: Libraries and distance education. | Information literacy—Web-based instruction. | Web-based instruction—Design. | Libraries—Special collections— Electronic information resources. | Libraries and community.
Classification: LCC Z718.85 .M86 2020 (print) | LCC Z718.85 (ebook) | DDC 025.5—dc23
LC record available at https://lccn.loc.gov/2020029647
LC ebook record available at https://lccn.loc.gov/2020029648

ISBN: 978-1-4408-6175-8 (paperback)
       978-1-4408-6176-5 (ebook)

24  23  22  21      2  3  4  5

This book is also available as an eBook.

Libraries Unlimited
An Imprint of ABC-CLIO, LLC

ABC-CLIO, LLC
147 Castilian Drive
Santa Barbara, California 93117
www.abc-clio.com

This book is printed on acid-free paper ∞

Manufactured in the United States of America

# Contents

# Figures and Tables

# Preface

This book was written right before the emergence of COVID-19 and the resulting pandemic that forced a sudden transition of our entire country, and most of our world, to online education over the span of just a few weeks. It is easy to imagine the explosion in educational technology, digital resources, and online pedagogies that will arise from this rapid change. At this moment in spring 2020, every library employee is supporting an online library and every librarian is practicing online librarianship. It seems highly likely that this shift to online learning will have long-term impacts on the way we deliver library services for the foreseeable future, even once we transition back to a new normal that again includes on-site instruction. As educators and students grow familiar with virtual and hybrid modalities and an increasing number of people look to reeducate and redeploy themselves throughout the economy, online learning will expand faster and farther than previously projected. This book is designed to help all of us experiencing online librarianship through trial-by-fire to continue supporting, educating, and connecting online learners in the most thoughtful, collaborative, and sustainable way far into the future. The three themes of this book—facilitating access, creating community, and building engagement—are crucial to the work we have ahead of us.

This begins with a careful evaluation of what services and resources your library currently provides, how well those are working, and for whom. It is also important to understand if users know about these services and how they find out about them. Sharing data, analyzing results, and building initiatives that help the library meet perceived gaps in services, resources, and outreach are the next step. Performing this process collaboratively with all library employees, along with campus and community stakeholders, will ensure the entire organization is invested in the outcome, while building internal knowledge and strengthening connections to our patrons.

Expanding access to resources and assistance, where it's needed and to the widest set of users possible, is the foundation of online librarianship. Ensuring the right eResources are available and enhancing discovery of these through better search interfaces and enhanced metadata are the building blocks of that foundation. Adding OER and open access content to your catalog and helping faculty create, discover, share, and integrate open resources into their teaching builds on that access in a way that improves equity and outcomes for all students.

Facilitating communication and community is challenging in an online environment—something recent events has taught all of us. However, research has shown us that peer interaction, eMentoring, and leveraging digital communication tools help. Making communication easy, convenient, and mobile improves engagement while reframing students' perception of social and digital media as a possible conduit for scholarly and professional interaction. As inclusive, discipline-agnostic centers of communities and campuses, libraries are well placed to support peer connections through virtual services like peer reference, peer tutoring, or eMentorships. Peer services lessen library anxiety in learners while also expanding virtual work and internship opportunities for fully online students and new professionals. Librarians know how to create, strengthen, and sustain diverse communities of users—this knowledge is critical to the success of online learning groups and cohorts, who need community to deepen learning and stay motivated.

Library, media, and information literacy instruction is performed by all librarians in all types of libraries. As we've learned, adapting these lessons to an online environment takes thoughtful planning. But technology offers us invaluable opportunities to apply literacy lessons in real time, directly to learners' everyday lives and goals as students, professionals, scholars, and creators. Harnessing tools that enhance collaborative and creative processes help us engage students in their learning while building their literacy, technology, and communication skills. Understanding the prevalent characteristics of your learner populations and ensuring they see the value of what you're teaching makes all the difference.

The transition to online librarianship, the evaluation of all library services and resources, and the challenge of communicating and engaging with online learners in new virtual environments may seem overwhelming. But remember, you're not doing it alone. Right now, everywhere, library and information professionals are seeking to understand what virtual services people need and want. We are working to improve access and discovery to resources across digital platforms. We are forging connections within local and global communities to promote learning, wellness, and cooperation. And we are leveling up the technology skills required to do all of this successfully. I hope you will use this book in the spirit it was written—as a useful tool for navigating an emerging professional and organizational paradigm that removes the stigma of distance and recognizes that all learners are potentially online learners and that all librarians are potentially, and perhaps now by necessity, online librarians.

# Acknowledgments

This book has been in the making for about fifteen years. That's when I started taking online classes at my local junior college, trying to finish a degree while working full time. My favorite class was an online world history course for which the instructor had built their own website with flashing GIFs, green links on a yellow background, and more pixelated clip art images than I could count. It was obviously a labor of love. And it was the first class where I spent more time learning the materials and interacting with the instructor than worrying about if I would make it to campus on time, where I would park, what I would wear, what kind of socially awkward conversations I would have with fellow students I didn't have time to get to know, or if I would have to speak aloud in class and potentially embarrass myself. Fifteen years ago is when I figured out online learning was for me. It took a few more years to find my calling in libraries, but when I did, supporting online education and virtual services became my focus.

In 2020, the need for libraries to support online learning went from one of many important topics in librarianship to its most critical question as COVID-19 swept the globe. Online education has now become a crucial tool in ensuring personal health and safety. It is clear that virtualizing services for online learners will be a priority for the foreseeable future. I hope this book helps library and information services professionals to expand and improve the services they are currently providing in a way that further increases access, community, and engagement with library resources and services.

Throughout my education and career, I have had the pleasure of working with and learning from many amazing folks in libraries and in online education. Some of them are cited in this book. This book is also built on the experience, research, and scholarship of librarians and educators who I don't personally know but who have inspired me through their work and writing. I'm humbled by the opportunity to add them to my reference lists.

Some individuals who need to be called out by name are Ruth Huard, Mark Adams, and Corey Gin for introducing me to the world of online instructional design and the social justice aspects of online learning. Debbie Faires and Dale David for hiring me to teach faculty to teach online, which provided endless insights into some very real struggles regarding engaging online students (and herding cats). Tom Bickley, the first librarian who invited me to teach information literacy, both online and in a library classroom. I also want to thank Mallory Debartolo for keeping me radical in my thinking about everything and Rae Ann Stahl for making me do things before I believed I could do things, like running an IT department or a library.

On a more personal note, I'd like to acknowledge Sharon Thompson and Adriana Poo who always provide on-demand support, more feedback than I ask for, and buy me coffee so I can keep working even when I forget my wallet. Jessica Gribble, the ever-patient editor who "gently nudged" me just enough times that I actually finished this. And finally Martin Mune, who provided the snacks, phone chargers, printer paper, and moral support to make this happen. When I told him he was like Lucia Moniz to my Colin Firth in *Love, Actually*, he just replied: "Yeah, you're a writer."

# Introduction

Online learning has the power to make education more equitable. It can mitigate barriers imposed by geography, economic and family responsibilities, time constraints, or health and mobility issues. It can make knowledge truly free, with just an Internet or mobile network connection. Online education brings people from all over the world, and right next door, together in a learning community full of promise and potential. Online learning describes both formal, structured education programs and the cognitive work most of our users do every day as they navigate the fire hydrant of information available on the Internet. It can also be isolating, frustrating, and demoralizing. Libraries have an integral part to play in supporting online education's opportunities and in meeting its challenges.

I began my career as an online instructional design assistant in a small "eCampus" department of two people, responsible for supporting a large public university of 30,000 students. Reams of forms and boxes of envelopes used in paper correspondence courses were stored in my cubicle, as paper-based distance education had been discontinued only a year or two before I was hired. It was 2008.

Three years later, every course section created on that campus had an online shell in the learning management system, we hosted six fully-online degree programs with hundreds of students enrolled, and I was working on a grant to extend online education to women in rural Pakistan. Nothing changed until everything did.

I learned a couple of very important lessons in that position that have proven true over the subsequent decade:

- Online education creates opportunities for students who don't have enough of them.
- Online education inspires some educators while it scares others.
- Online education requires its own instructional design.

- Online education is the most sustainable way we have right now to provide education to anyone who wants it.

This book speaks to these lessons in three overarching themes: access, community, and engagement.

## Access

Throughout this book you will find an emphasis on access. Providing users access to the content they need or want, where they are most likely to look for it. Access to librarian or peer assistance through communication portals learners are comfortable and familiar with. The need to incorporate open access, open educational resources, and linked open data into our everyday library practices to ensure learners have required resources, regardless of their affiliations or status. Access to learning materials in a variety of formats that may be utilized by people of all learning styles and abilities. And, finding ways to provide local resource and space to online learners getting help from your on-site library.

Another lesson imparted to me, this time while as an online learning librarian, is that many administrators and executives believe online education is the best way for their organization to make money. The challenges of that could fill an entire book of their own, but I add it here because of the impact this belief and expectation has on people supporting online learners. Specifically, that institutions frequently put online learners into buckets based on how or what they pay, not necessarily by what they need. This often leads to an inequity of access to resources and services, such as school or university librarians and libraries, among different groups of online learners. This book attempts to equip librarians with tools to address this inequity using sustainable methods. If online learners cannot access the resources or services they need, if there are inequities between online and on-site leaners, you're not done yet.

## Community

Libraries are a natural builder of communities. Academic, public, and school libraries all strive to establish ourselves as safe, inclusive spaces that support knowledge building and creative activities for everyone. This function should be maintained in virtual spaces as well as it is in physical ones. Online librarians embrace this principle by teaching tools that support collaboration and online community interaction. They may also develop peer services that expand opportunities to help and teach online patrons while leveraging the benefits of peer learning; or create eMentorship programs that establish meaningful relationships in virtual spaces. Hosting and facilitating community groups of lifelong learners taking an online course together is another way libraries support online learning.

Librarians also forge ties across organizational lines in support of online learners. Building partnerships between teaching faculty, course coordinators, instructional designers, researchers, administrators, technology vendors, and student advocates ensures online learners have a whole community working toward their success. As discipline-agnostic educators dedicated to the dissemination of knowledge, librarians are uniquely situated in many educational organizations to build this web of support.

## Engagement

Digital and information literacy go hand in hand when providing instruction and reference assistance to online learners. Building instructional activities that relate to users' own lives and goals is critical to both the online or on-site learning experiences, but with online learners, engagement is even more crucial. There are just too many distractions and other sources of non-authoritative information for them to turn to. We need to grab their attention, make them care, get them talking to each other—all while equipping them with a diverse set of technology tools that will make their online learning experience more impactful and relevant for their future success. This book posits that interactive, technology-enhanced learning activities optimally placed in the learner pathway is the right kind of instructional design for online library-, information-, and digital-literacy instruction.

The civil rights activist Bayard Rustin once said: "We need, in every community, a group of angelic troublemakers." In online education's evolving landscape, librarians, with their specialized information expertise and professional ethos, are well poised to play the angelic troublemaker, agitating for greater consideration and support of online learning. When we demand open, free digital access for all learners to the information sources they need, librarians know exactly what that entails and the impact it will have. When librarians apply our expertise at community building, we establish strong, inclusive bonds of inquiry, professional development, and scholarship. And when we seek to actively engage learners, librarians do so with a deep understanding that every user is a unique individual with diverse learner needs and expectations. The challenge online librarianship meets head-on is applying the principles, expertise, and energy libraries bring to the table into the online sphere in the ways that best provide meaningful support to online learners.

# PART 1

# Facilitating Access

# What Is Online Librarianship?

## Introduction

Online learning is growing. In higher education, K–12, corporate training, professional development, and personal enrichment, enrollment in online and hybrid courses, degree programs, microcredentials, and massive open online courses (MOOCs) continues to increase. At the same time, the variety of modes and platforms that online learners engage in multiply and evolve at a rapid pace. Despite the rise and fall of buzzwords and instructional technology giants, online learning is not a fad any educator can ignore. Librarians and information professionals must tune into the needs of online learners in order to help the over 33 percent of postsecondary students enrolled in an online course, the 58 percent of high schools with completely online courses, adult learners in 630 microcredential programs, and the one hundred million MOOC participants (Johnson, 2019; Lederman, 2018; NCES, 2019). For academic librarians it is especially important to note that while postsecondary enrollment has decreased overall between 2010 and 2019, the actual number of students in online courses has increased. Growth in higher education is coming from online programs.

For libraries to support online education, those responsible for library services must reorientate themselves to the distinct needs of online learners. Online learners may have varying degrees of connection with a physical campus, classroom, or peer populations. These learners may be completing schoolwork at any hour of the day, due to location, responsibilities, or preferences. Some will work via desktop or laptop, and others will mostly participate using their mobile devices. They'll have different backgrounds, digital and information literacy skills, language preferences, and expectations than on-campus students. They may not be traditionally matriculated students, relying on local academic and public libraries with resources and access privileges distinct from on-campus students. They may be in rural areas or countries with varying degrees of infrastructure. The Internet may be their only source of information, and that Internet connection could have bandwidth limitations or be available only certain times of the day or week. Many will need assistance establishing a peer group or learning community for support. The practice of online librarianship, as described in this book, works to address these differences in the way reference, instruction, communication, collection management, and assessment are developed and delivered so that online learners are central to the design of these services, rather than an exception, afterthought, or footnote.

## Online Learning vs. Distance Learning

Throughout this book you will find an intentional preference for the term "online" over the term "distance": online education, online learners, online instruction, online librarian. First, "distance" is often a misnomer. It is not necessarily proximity (or lack thereof) to a campus that influences the choice to learn online. Second, the preference for the term "online" over distance reflects a desire to remove or negate the privilege of proximity from our way of thinking about education. The term "distance" potentially reinforces the unneeded separation of students learning online from those learning in a physical, on-site classroom. Bayne, Gallagher, and Lamb (2014) tell us: "The term 'distance education' is itself a negative definition—'distance' education is what is not on-campus; it is discursively determined and at the same time de-privileged via an explicitly spatial orientation which constitutes it as other to the 'norm' of the on-campus" (570). This is particularly troublesome when potential employers, college admission boards, and even the academic institution the online program is hosted at makes distinctions in pricing, access, benefits, and privileges between traditional on-campus education and online education. This discrepancy may affect students' ability to receive faculty assistance, award eligibility, access to resources, and graduate program acceptance. For faculty, distance education contributions may be counted differently toward tenure and promotion. For job seekers, distance education degrees may be weighted differently than on-campus degrees, creating serious disadvantages for students without the socioeconomic means or physical capabilities to attend on-campus.

Although changing the term to online may not seem significant—online education can be considered deprivileged as well—it is a more accurate representation of mode. Distance education does not describe students in a program or hosting institution or organization that is completely online. They are not distant from any particular place, as there is no place to be. It also does not accurately represent the condition of students attending both on-campus and online or hybrid courses from the same institution. They are not at a distance, simply choosing to attend virtually rather than physically for a variety of reasons. Online is a more inclusive term, intended to reorientate our focus on the virtual aspects of the learning rather than the learner's physical situation. For high schools, colleges, and universities, it is important to not make distinctions between students who attend on-campus versus online to ensure all students feel enfranchised and part of the institution's life and legacy. This increases students' overall satisfaction with their education and experience, thus improving retention and performance. It also makes for lasting alumni connections that can be critical to the financial health of an institution. Occasionally, especially when evaluating services such as mail delivery of physical resources, the term "distance" should be carefully applied to indicate a geographic barrier to access. However, if a service is beneficial to someone living 50 miles away, it may also be beneficial to someone with limited mobility, no time to come to campus, or an individual who lives 20 miles away but has no transportation access. It's wise to be wary of the distance signifier generally and what arbitrary and potentially harmful categories it may be putting learners into.

## Online Librarianship or Embedded Librarianship

Considering the wide range of online learning modalities and the ubiquity of online learning, it is clear that no one style of librarianship can adequately encompass the needs of all online learners. Embedded librarianship is a proven pedagogical practice, a set of behaviors and services describing one type of online learning support. It describes a method of librarianship in which the librarian becomes an integral part of a course, from design to support to assessment. It requires intense partnerships with the course instructor and/or team and the time to be an active member of the learning experience throughout. It is a valuable and innovative practice. And like many pedagogical practices, it is not always possible, applicable, or scalable.

Supporting online learner types and modalities takes a large wheelhouse of pedagogical approaches, best practices, assessment methods, and consultations with specific and diverse user groups. What this book hopes to do is orientate all information professionals to the needs of online learners and guide them in finding the right kinds of services, provided in the most sustainable methods, in the best platforms for the users, at the right time in the learning process. That includes but is not limited to embedded librarianship. Let's start this orientation to the online learner by taking a bird's-eye view of the online education landscape, to get a better understanding of what we're working with.

## Online Education Landscape

As online education has grown to fit the needs of students, instructors, and organizations, it has taken on many forms. This section provides a basic overview of the most prevalent modalities for online education.

### Flipped or Inverted Courses

In flipped or inverted courses, students will often watch videos, review content, complete exercises, and discuss issues online that prepare them for in-class practice and coaching. This optimizes class time for student-instructor or student-student interactions, including working with example problems, going over the most difficult concepts or sticking points, and getting in-person feedback. Flipped classes have proven to be very effective in teaching difficult math and engineering concepts and are being adapted outside the STEM fields, as well. Librarians have been experimenting with flipping the information literacy classroom, for both on-site and online sessions, by asking learners to watch tutorials or complete searching activities beforehand. This refocuses instruction away from tool-teaching marathons toward informed discussions and interactive question-and-answer sessions.

To support flipped classrooms, making sure learners have access to the materials and providing supporting materials on difficult concepts is important. Libraries may be asked to host instructional videos, clear copyright on video and digital content, or purchase streaming content to support flipped instruction. Providing guidance on closed captioning and accessibility could also fall under the library's purview, depending on the campus resources available.

### Hybrid and Web-Enhanced Courses

Courses in a hybrid modality generally have a reduced amount of face-to-face time, with some lectures, interactions, or activities taking place online. Hybrid can indicate a class group meets every other week, only for proctored exams, or for a single introductory session at the beginning of the term. This is also sometimes referred to as "blended." This modality offers some flexibility for the instructor(s) and students while providing physical spaces for orientation, testing, discussion, and in-person help.

Web-enhanced courses are in-person courses that utilize online resources such as a learning management system (LMS), websites, or social media sites to provide 24/7 access to content, quizzes, discussions, instructor help, etc.

For these course types libraries may need to assist instructors with content hosting, and copyright and accessibility issues, similar to flipped courses. Librarians may need to create tutorials or offer assisting in accessing content off-site or using technology platforms. Online information literacy instruction and virtual research assistance are provided by librarians or peer experts via online chat; an LMS discussion board or social media hashtag will hopefully be part of the "enhanced" portion of the class, as well.

## Online or Distance Courses

As of 2020, most universities and over half of all high schools offer fully online courses. These could be in a variety of subjects, from general education courses, to popular electives, to smaller graduate or AP courses in specialized fields. An online course is fully web-based, usually through an LMS where content is organized in "modules" by week or section. Within the LMS, students will likely read or watch lectures, take quizzes or exams that may be timed or randomized, and engage in discussion threads. Frequently, the library has a presence in the LMS, be it a link to the library's website, a search box for the library catalog, a module with information literacy instruction for the learners, a subject or course LibGuide, or an embedded librarian that answers questions in near real time. Some students may still be able to come to campus and the library for help or access to resources. These learners are more likely to have peers they can turn to for help, but those peers may not be very knowledgeable on the subject. Making sure students know where credible information and help are available, be it from librarians, peers, or electronic resources, will be key to supporting these courses.

## Synchronous vs. Asynchronous

Online courses are often distinguished by another factor—synchronous or asynchronous. This is true for courses within a diploma or degree program at an accredited school or university as well as elected online courses for professional training, skill development, or lifelong learning from organizations such as Udacity, Udemy, or Codecademy.

A synchronous course is completed along a set timeline, often requiring live meetings held with web conference software such as Skype, Zoom, WebEx, or Google Hangouts. Instructors, teaching assistants, and/or peers likely actively engage in discussion, grading, and feedback throughout the course. Some learners find synchronous classes more motivating as the group is moving along a learning path together, with discussions and Q&As happening in real time. However, those with rigid schedules and multiple priorities or learners unsure of their time commitments will frequently steer clear of synchronous courses.

Asynchronous courses may follow a timeline with set due dates for assignments and quizzes, but no live meetings are required. The student is able to fulfill all course obligations via email, the LMS, or message boards. Self-paced online courses allow students to work completely at their own pace, with no deadlines at all. These course types frequently do not offer instructor interaction but instead have computer-graded assignments and exams. They likely also have message boards where peers can discuss the content or questions in their own time.

## Online and Hybrid Diploma and Degree Programs

Increasingly, K–12 institutions, colleges, and universities are initiating online or hybrid degree programs in which a cohort will meet once or twice a year while completing the bulk of their coursework and research online. This is an especially popular modality for professional graduate degrees such as library and information science, nursing, and education administration. They may be labeled "online programs," although they do require infrequent meetings. If at all possible, a librarian should schedule an instruction or orientation session during the introductory meeting of such programs to ensure students are familiar with resources and understand their access privileges. Holding and advertising open office hours during cohort meetings on campus can also be very useful. For the rest of the year when students are virtual, troubleshooting access to electronic and print materials, assisting in the discovery and evaluation of research materials, providing virtual reference services and connecting students to grant, career, and professional development resources will be critical. Emphasis on creating relevant, quick, easy-to-use online content will help manage the workload in supporting these programs. Building close working relationships with faculty, course designers, and coordinators in these programs is recommended.

## Online Certificates and Continuing Education

Similar to the online or hybrid degree programs, a growing number of institutions offer online certificates or continuing education units for professionals. Unfortunately, it's more likely with these programs that the participants will not be traditionally matriculated students and therefore have limited access to the library's electronic and print resources. It may also be the case that such certificate programs do not have a designated liaison librarian, making workload management even more difficult and complex. Again, relevant, short, concise online content outlining access privileges, connecting students to local libraries, and linking to quality online resources for professional development or career questions will help tremendously. Advocating for your learners in online programs by negotiating publisher agreements and database subscriptions to include them as regularly licensed users is another possible tact.

## Massive Open Online Courses

Massive open online courses, or MOOCs, emerged in the late 2000s as a new modality in online learning emphasizing large courses open to all learners that relied on connected learning and information sharing with peers for content mastery. MOOCs have since evolved into a wide range of formats offered by a large variety of organizations. These include:

- Synchronous and asynchronous cohort courses, as well as self-paced courses.

- Courses for high school or college credit, offered by academic institutions or school districts.

- Courses offering continuing education credit, required for certain professions.

- Courses offering skill enhancement for learners seeking specific skills or certifications to level up careers, especially in technology sectors. These courses may be part of micro- or nanodegree programs (discussed later in this section) offered by MOOC platforms in partnerships with corporations or government agencies.

- Open, free courses on a variety of topics from math and engineering to arts and humanities. These may be offered by academic institutions, nonprofits, or for-profit platforms that offer tiered payment systems.

Library support of MOOCs will vary greatly depending on if the MOOC is for credit, professional development, or personal enrichment. Public librarians will find models for building learning communities and supporting MOOC learners later in this book. Creating comfortable, safe spaces, encouraging peer support, and providing technology assistance are necessary building blocks to this endeavor. Academic librarians responsible for departments or programs utilizing MOOCs for instruction will find more information on providing services to large courses in later chapters, as well. A focus on peer learning and peer mentorship, FAQs, social media, and easy-to-use instructional materials supporting transferable research skills will be key to success in this area. Librarians working for corporations and nonprofits will want to know the various platforms and what each has to offer in way of skill attainment. They can also utilize MOOC platforms to build tailored training courses in partnership with organizational trainers and instructional designers.

## Badging, Nanodegrees, and Microcredentialing

Another emerging online learning modality is a twist on the badging fad of the last decade known as microcredentialing. Here we will use microcredentialing as a term to encompass the nanogedrees, microdegrees, and badges offered by MOOC platforms, nonprofit and for-profit organizations, and licensing agencies. Microcredentials can be thought of as badges awarded to learners that complete a small amount of courses or credit units usually aligned to address a specific skill set. The education and technology sectors have been leading microcredentialing pilots. Udacity and AT&T created a nanodegree program including Python and Java coding skills that feeds AT&T's internship program. North Carolina State University's Friday Institute designed fifteen microcredentials for teacher education, which participants have found immediately applicable to their teaching (DeMonte, 2017). Librarians at any institution working with or supporting microcredentialing will likely need to work on digital literacy content for reentry students and new learners with limited tech skills, encouraging peer-to-peer learning, and FAQ building.

## Keeping Informed

As methods of teaching and learning online multiply and evolve, it is important for librarians and other information professionals to remain current in the latest standards, approaches, modes, and tools used. This allows for informed selections of materials and platforms, deployment of best practices, and helps us reach and teach online learners most effectively. Although it may seem daunting to keep up with every fad or trend, it's really a matter of checking in with the right professional guidelines and publications, keeping in contact with your peers, and having lots of discussions with your target audiences. Below is a brief selection of professional standards as well as print and online publications and conferences for librarians supporting online education.

### Guidelines and Standards

- The American Library Association's (ALA) American Association of School Librarians (AASL) offers standards to assist school library practitioners in supporting learning of all kinds and the use of Open Educational Resources (OER). The AASL *Standards Framework for Learners* includes standards for learners, school librarians, and school libraries. These will help school library information professionals map lessons, activities, and assessments to competencies such as Think, Create, Share, and Grow by building skills in inquiry, inclusion, collaboration, curation, exploration, and engagement. In November 2019, AASL released their OER Toolkit that provides support for school librarians with the creation and curation of OER at a school, district, or state level, increasing the quality digital resources available for online learning.

- The ALA's Association of College and Research Libraries (ACRL) publishes a variety of standards and tools to guide academic libraries in supporting online services, such as the *Standards for Distance Learning Library Services*, most recently updated in 2016. These standards touch on resources, services, facilities, staffing, and the management of all these functions. ACRL also offers best practices for distance library instruction, instruction collaboration, and criteria for successful assessment programs for online instruction.

- The National Standards for Quality Online Learning have been a national benchmark for K–12 online programs and courses since 2007. As of 2020, these standards are undergoing revision by Quality Matters and the Virtual Learning Leaderships Alliance with the hopes of developing an openly licensed set of standards for the evaluation of online K–12 learning.

- Quality Matters (QM) offers a well-respected and established peer-review process to evaluate and improve the quality of online and hybrid courses. QM is a membership-funded organization that provides professional development, webinars, course reviews, and rubrics for online educators and course designers. Some basic rubrics and evaluation tools are available for free to nonmembers.

- The Reference and User Services Association (RUSA), also of ALA, offers libraries *Guidelines for Implementing and Maintaining Virtual Reference Services*. These guidelines, updated in 2017, define virtual reference and provide guidance on training, providing, and managing virtual reference services.

## Publications and Conferences

- *Campus Technology*, a professional publication available both online and in print since 2004, provides hands-on, practical information regarding technology trends and practices for educators, administrators, and IT and information professionals in higher education.

- *The Chronicle of Higher Education*, an established professional publication, covers college and university news and issues, including frequent reviews and analysis of emerging online learning initiatives and programs. Some content is available free online, full access possibly available from a college or university library near you.

- Code{4}Lib offers national and local conferences for library technologists, programmers, and developers as well as a monthly journal in publication since 2007. This grassroots organization also offers an active technology support community via its listserv.

- *EducauseReview* and *EducauseQuarterly* are both published by Educause, one of the largest and most established organizations for information technology in higher education. These are open access, online publications that offer insights into the latest IT trends and how they affect higher education and educators. Educause also holds well-attended annual meetings on technology in education.

- *eLearn Magazine* is an open access, peer-reviewed publication available free online. It seeks to provide evidence-based guidance for practical applications in blended and online learning within the K–12, higher education, nonprofit, and governmental spheres.

- *The Electronic Journal of e-Learning* is an open access, peer-reviewed journal indexed by Scopus and Thomas Reuters. Published since 2003, EJEL focuses on pedagogical topics related to the implementation, analysis, and management of e-learning initiatives.

- Electronic Resources and Libraries is a highly-regarded annual conference for information professionals focused on ways to improve and expand the collection, management, and accessibility of electronic resources and digital collections.

- *Information Today, Inc.* holds various library and digital learning conferences, including the well-known Computers in Libraries annual event in Washington, DC, and the Internet Librarian conference held each year in Monterey, California. These events focus on virtual and digital services, online learning design and tools, web design, and emerging technologies.

- The *Internet Reference Services Quarterly* is a peer-reviewed journal started in 1996 that seeks to keep information professionals and educators up to date on emerging technologies as they relate to information discovery, access, and assistance. The journal emphasizes theoretical, research, and practical applications.

- The *Journal of Library and Information Services in Distance Learning* is a peer-reviewed journal publishing research articles, theoretical papers, case studies, and book reviews related to librarianship in distance learning since 2004. The annual conference proceedings of the Distance Library Services Conference are also published here. The Distance Library Services Conference was established in 1982 and continues to draw librarians, educators, and instructional designers interested in distance and online library services.

- The *Journal of Web Librarianship* provides the latest research and practical reviews on topics such as web design, library integration with web applications, and the future of web librarianship. It is a peer-reviewed Taylor and Francis publication started in 2007.

- LibTech is an annual conference hosted by Macalester College in St. Paul Minnesota for over a decade. It is devoted to providing library professionals a place to discuss, learn, and experience the latest technologies influencing library services and spaces.

- The *Online Information Review* offers research, reviews, and analysis of search engines, databases, interface design, and intelligence agents as related to web searching. Published since 1980, OIR is peer-reviewed and emphasizes the computer/information science perspective.

- The *Online Learning Journal* is an open access, peer-reviewed journal from the Online Learning Consortium. Scholars and professionals discuss practices, issues, and theories related to online learning for K–12 and higher education. Additionally, the not-for-profit Online Learning Consortium offers a wealth of expert reports and best practice literature online, as well as national conferences and regional events around digital learning in higher education.

- *THE (Technology Horizons in Education) Journal* is a professional publication focused on technology in K–12 education since 1972. It's targeted at educators, technologists, and high-level administrators who engage in program planning and determine policies.

## Conclusion

It is imperative that library professionals familiarize themselves with the expanding online education landscape. Online learning spans all library types. Online learners are high school students in AP classes, undergrads in online degree programs, working professionals seeking microcredentials, and individuals seeking personal enrichment in large open access courses. Learners and educators in all these modalities look to libraries for help discovering, accessing, understanding, evaluating, utilizing, and sharing resources. Designing instruction, reference, collection management, communication tools, and assessments for and in conversation with online learners and educators is essential to meeting the needs of a significantly growing portion of our users and to remaining relevant in this changing education landscape.

## References

Bayne, Sian, Michael Sean Gallagher, and James Lamb. 2014. "Being 'at' University: The Social Topologies of Distance Students." *Higher Education* 67(5): 569–583.

DeMonte, Jenny. 2017. *Micro-Credentials for Teachers: What Three Early Adopter States Have Learned So Far.* Washington, DC: American Institute for Research.

Johnson, Sydney. 2019. "Much Ado about MOOCs: Where Are We in the Evolution of Online Courses?" *EdSurge*. https://www.edsurge.com/news/2019 -02-26-much-ado-about-moocs-where-are-we-in-the-evolution-of -online-courses.

Lederman, Doug. 2018. "Online Education Ascends." *Inside Higher Ed.* https://
    www.insidehighered.com/digital-learning/article/2018/11/07/new-data
    -online-enrollments-grow-and-share-overall-enrollment.
National Center for Education Statistics. 2019. *Characteristics of Public and Private
    Elementary and Secondary Schools in the United States: Results from the 2017–
    18 National Teacher and Principal Survey First Look.* https://nces.ed.gov
    /pubs2019/2019140.pdf.

# CHAPTER TWO

# Understand How You Help: Evaluating Services to Online Learners

## Introduction

Although you can begin applying the strategies described in this book to your services immediately, it is strongly recommended to start with a programmatic review of your library's services to online learners. (The term "services" here is used to encompass a broad range of library services and resources provided to online users, including eResources and digital tools.) Such a review, generally referred to as a needs assessment or gap analysis, will guide the organization in prioritizing, implementing, managing, and evaluating the changes and improvements it invests in. An inclusive, intentional review process that focuses on user input and an honest assessment of services will lay the groundwork for building stakeholder partnerships across your campus and/or community, educating library employees on the tenets of online education, and hopefully encourage a culture of evaluation and reflection in the library.

The organization may conduct the needs assessment through multiple rounds, depending on how deeply it desires to understand users' needs and how granular the organization wants to get with the individual populations it serves. These may include undergraduates, graduate students, K–12 students, lifelong learners, international students, distance-only students, continuing education professionals, and returning students. Once completed, the results can be expressed and disseminated in a SWOT or possibly SOAR or SCORE analysis that will lead the organization in identifying current service gaps or challenges and setting aspirational goals based on collected data and user input.

## Components of a Needs Assessment

The Association of College and Research Libraries (ACRL) provides standards for services that are required for equitable access to libraries for online students. Originally drafted in 2008, the *Standards for Distance Learning Library Services* were more recently revised in 2016. Building on Herbert's (2016) four main components of distance learning assessment, a programmatic review of services to online learners will include:

1. Identifying online courses, programs, degrees, cohorts, and populations the library is expected to serve. Understanding the size and demographic makeup of these populations. Identifying online education collaborators, likely instructors, instructional designers, or teaching assistants and understanding their library service needs.

2. Inventorying the services provided to online learners, and identifying who in the library is responsible for their provision and what the expected service levels are for distance and online populations.

3. Measuring the awareness of library services among online learners and instructors leading online classes, programs, and cohorts. Understanding what promotional work has already been done and its impact on awareness.

4. Assessing online learners' satisfaction with library services. Developing methods to assess the impact of instruction and reference efforts to online learners and tracking outcomes as improvements are made.

These components combine to create a powerful image of what your library does for online learners, if they are aware of what you offer, and how well these services and resources work for them. First, who are your users and what do they need? Second, what do you provide compared to what the users need or what distance learning guidelines, such as the ACRL standards, indicate is required? The key here is to identify the gaps. Once this is established, strategies for filling the gaps can be devised, programs revitalized, and resources procured (hopefully). However, new and improved resources and services will matter little if the users they benefit don't know they exist. That's why measuring the awareness of library services among online learners and instructors and understanding the best way to communicate or locate services, according to them, is critical. Assessing satisfaction and awareness will potentially be both the first phase and last phase of the

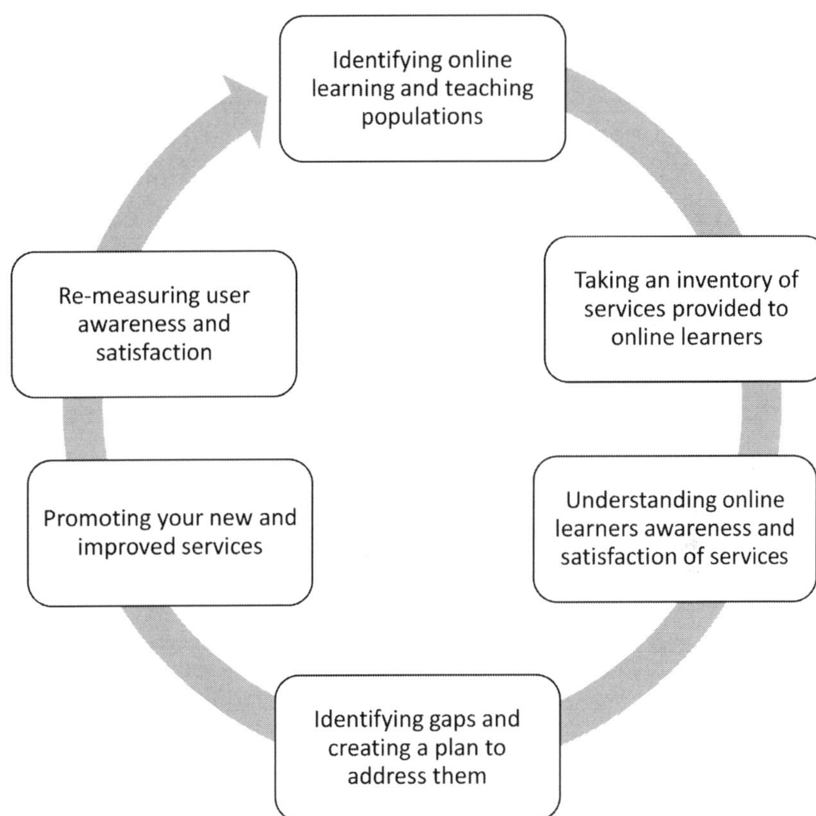


**Figure 2.1**   Online learner needs assessment cycle.

assessment. An accurate account of online user satisfaction gives the organization a baseline from which to improve and measure success. Because the student cohort will likely change between a pre- and postsurvey of this magnitude (say an entire campus or community online learner survey), it is difficult to accurately measure learning outcomes. But satisfaction and self-efficacy can certainly be tracked with authority. Figure 2.1 illustrates the proposed cycle.

This chapter equips you with tools to begin a service inventory and needs assessment. It also suggests methods for organizing your evaluation and summarizing the information for dissemination. In-depth explorations of reviewing specific services and resources for online learners and strategies for improving them are delineated in later chapters. To illustrate the value of performing this evaluation, let's look at a case study from Kansas State University (KSU) Libraries evidencing the effectiveness of this process.

## KSU Libraries' Longitudal Study

Pitts, Coleman, and Conella (2013), the KSU Libraries' Distance Education Team, provide an excellent example of an academic library applying the iterative process of needs assessment to evaluating its online learning support in their 2011–2014 longitudinal study of KSU Library services to online learning populations. Their initial 2011 survey was sent to over 8,000 students taking classes online and 388 online instructors, which the KSU researchers refer to as "distance" users. The survey was designed to evaluate the student and faculty awareness of library resources and services for distance education, the extent to which students and educators used them, and their perceived usefulness. The survey asked respondents to report awareness, usage, and usefulness on a 1–5 Likert scale. The tool asked how aware users were of:

- KSU Libraries has web-based help pages, including a page specifically for distance learners.

- If a distance learner needs a resource (book, article, video, CD, map, etc.) that KSU Libraries do not own, KSU Libraries will attempt to find it and deliver it.

- Distance learners can access KSU Libraries' databases from off-campus using any computer connected to the Internet.

- Distance learners can obtain immediate help from a librarian through online chat, telephone, or email during KSU Libraries' service hours.

It also asked users to rate the usefulness of resources and services such as:

- eJournals.
- RefWorks.
- Librarians help via chat, email, or telephone.
- Subject guides.
- Consultation or in-depth assistance.

And how frequently respondents used resources from:

- KSU State Libraries (all resources).
- Local public libraries.
- Local non-KSU academic libraries.
- Interlibrary loan.
- Free resources from the Internet.

Results indicated a critical need to increase marketing and improve awareness of library services available to off-campus students. Over half of distance students were unaware of most KSU Library services, as were nearly half of faculty teaching online. The vast majority of students used free resources from the Internet most frequently for research, nearly 50 percent more than used library resources (Pitts, Coleman, and Conella, 2013, n.p.). In response to the survey results, Kansas State Libraries met with campus online learning stakeholders to explore ways of increasing collaboration and visibility. The following improvements were made based on the survey and those collaboration discussions:

- Launched web-scale discovery platform with single search box.
- Restructured databases' pages to align with curriculum format.
- Improved interlibrary loan services.
- Prioritized chat reference by increasing service hours.
- Created a searchable FAQ database, with relevant entries tagged for distance learning.
- Initiated the use of LibGuides for online instruction.
- Created webpages delineating distance services specifically.
- Created librarian role in LMS to help online instructors feel more comfortable about adding them to their online course.
- Added a distance services section to their online course in the LMS.

Three years after the initial survey, the group again sent out questionnaires to nearly 5,000 students and 433 online instructors (Bonella, Pitts, and Coleman, 2017). Undergraduate and graduate students reported at least a 15 percent increase in familiarity with various library resources. The survey also found that a 14 percent increase in undergraduates reported they used the library "a lot," going from 11 to 25 percent during the three-year period the noted improvements were implemented (Bonella, Pitts, and Coleman, 2017, 74). And the number of online undergraduates that were very satisfied with library services went up from 15 to 34 percent during the same period. Graduate and faculty student responses indicated a similar increase in awareness and satisfaction (Bonella, Pitts, and Coleman, 2017, 75–76). So what can other libraries do to recreate this understanding, effort, and results in their own organization?

## Identifying Online Learners and Collaborators

In some ways, identifying your online learner populations and likely collaborators is a type of inventory. For academic libraries, what online programs, degrees, certificates, or courses does your university or school use? How large are those courses and cohorts? Who designs the courses, coordinates the sections, or teaches the classes? What kind of hybrid or web-enhanced courses are there? And are all courses assigned a course shell in the LMS, even on-campus sections? This is going to require a lot of reaching out to chairs, directors, coordinators, and department administrators. Accreditation, curriculum development, and course approval cycles might be great times to reach out to departments or committees to get this information. And be on the lookout for online programs that serve nonmatriculated students without library privileges.

School librarians will want to reach out to administrators locally and at the district level to understand if students may be taking hybrid, online, or MOOC courses in their districts and how many students elect them. What on-campus courses utilize online components that would benefit from library resources or services? Are there ways to reach out to those students and teachers specifically?

For special or corporate librarians, it's a question of what certifications, credentials, microdegrees or professional development are required for those they serve, and do these exist as online offerings? What are the possible modalities and platforms learners should access? Who is required or encouraged to attend and at what time in their career?

Public librarians may want to reach out to users that access online education resources, home-schooling populations, GED courses, test-prep courses, as well as those interested in technology literacy instruction. Many public libraries offer peer-learning opportunities for online learners, so an inventory will include any of those cohorts or those potentially interested in that programming.

## Taking a Service Inventory

Virtually all libraries do physical inventories at some point. Reconciling your physical inventory to your catalog, ensuring everything is in its correct location, adjusting location codes or availability status, replacing lost or stolen items, repairing damages materials—this is collection maintenance 101. Although we may not have time to do this often, it's a given that physical collections must be maintained in a regular manner or users will not be able to find what they need. In a similar manner, we review usage statistics and information currency for our print collections when weeding or shifting, making decisions regarding deaccessioning items, serials, or purchasing digital replacements for print items to increase access or usage. eResources and digital collections have been folded into these processes in the last few decades, as well. Increased data collection, standards for consistent usage statistics, and patron-driven acquisition programs for eBooks are commonplace in most libraries. Additionally, service desks and help transactions have also come under the assessment lens through the collection of transaction frequency, complexity, and user satisfaction. Based on this data, trends like reducing desk numbers, providing chat reference, or introducing 24/7 assistance have emerged. All of this happens alongside ethnographic research and studies on space and technology usage.

It's not a stretch to imagine applying similar assessment methods to better understanding the needs of online students and to increase our effectiveness at providing services and resources to online users. With the right tools and some potential processes to follow, assessing services to online learners doesn't need to be a monumental undertaking, but rather an enlightening, phased process that improves services and resources for all.

Again, building on the ACRL Standards as a guide, Table 2.1 highlights potential categories for your service inventory.

Of course, any inventory will need to be customized to your organization. However, there are some general categories reviewers will need in order to identify gaps and formulate action plans to address them. Table 2.2 provides a template that expands on these categories to help you plan. Asking multiple employees, at different levels of the organizations and all relevant departments, to complete the inventory will ensure all services and resources are reviewed. It will also help reveal inconsistencies or discrepancies in the service levels, definitions, and usage or turnaround expectations within the organization. Consider also inviting end users to complete the inventory for services they are familiar with.

## Methods of a Needs Assessment

A needs assessment is a process. This process allows us to identify gaps between what our organization should look like and what it actually does look like, along with what factors have led to this gap. With this information we can devise strategies and timelines to close the gaps and become the organization our users need now and will need in the near future. The needs assessment process should take place regularly. It is appropriate for a large-scale organizational review but also can be helpful with understanding a new or emerging user population or service paradigm.

A needs assessment is ideally performed using multiple modalities, including online survey and feedback activities, focus groups with different user groups, observations, analysis of available data, and an understanding of the current and future organizational landscape. Utilizing mixed methods allows for all populations to be consulted, collects a diversity of perspective, mitigates issues of self-reporting and bias, and increases possibility for engagement with your user community. It also provides an opportunity for as many people as possible to get involved in the assessment—performing it, contributing data to it, and analyzing it. If possible, engage frontline employees responsible for a service or resources to create and administer the assessment

**Table 2.1  Recommended Categories for a Library Service Inventory**

| Service Area | Service Aspects |
| --- | --- |
| eResources/ digital collections | • Streaming video (with captions)<br>• Online reference works<br>• eBooks and eTextbooks<br>• Demand- or patron-driven acquisition programs<br>• Databases serving general education curriculum<br>• Databases serving online programs/degrees<br>• Government publications and data resources<br>• Online study guides for GED, GRE, LSAT, MCAT, and SAT<br>• Online standards and manuals<br>• Local and state history works<br>• Common Core curriculum support<br>• Language learning resources<br>• Open access publications<br>• Course eReserves |
| Access | • Remote access to all resources, especially those resources listed above<br>• Ease and intuitiveness of remote access<br>• Point-of-need access help options<br>• Password reset options<br>• Point-of-need password help<br>• Alternatives to resources not available remotely<br>• Alternatives to resources not available for non-card-holding patrons or organization affiliates (nonmatriculated students)<br>• Physical material delivery to distant students |
| Reciprocal borrowing | • Visiting patron programs and agreements<br>• Interlibrary loan home delivery<br>• Consortia-borrowing home delivery |
| Copyright assistance | • Copyright guidance to faculty for eReserves or course content delivery through the LMS or online<br>• Open licensing guidance for faculty |
| Reference/ research consultation | • Provision of point-of-need reference—live chat<br>• Provision of point-of-need reference—web<br>• Provision of point-of-need reference—LMS<br>• Provision of point-of-need reference—email<br>• Provision of point-of-need reference—social media<br>• Provision of phone reference<br>• Provision of online office hours, scheduled or open hours |

*(continued)*

**Table 2.1**   (*continued*)

| Service Area | Service Aspects |
| --- | --- |
| Information and digital literacy instruction | • Online instructional content—videos/GIFs<br>• Online instructional content—subject guides<br>• Online instructional content—course guides<br>• Online instructional content—LMS<br>• Online instructional content—social media<br>• Online tutorials dedicated to online course sections or programs<br>• Online tutorials reviewing remote access<br>• Availability of tailored online instruction sessions, synchronous<br>• Availability of tailored online instruction sessions, asynchronous<br>• Online introductory sessions to online cohorts<br>• Integration of librarians into online programs, courses, and curriculum planning<br>• PDF alternatives to online multimedia instructional content |
| Community/ connection | • Provision of liaison, school, or adult learning librarians for online programs, courses, or cohorts<br>• Consistency of assigned librarians throughout course or program<br>• Video conferencing and instant messaging during reference and help transactions<br>• Use of LMS discussion threads<br>• Use of social media to communicate/interact with learners<br>• Availability of peer learning services and spaces<br>• Availability of eMentoring program |
| Environment/ tools | • Usability and currency of library's webpages and guides<br>• Usability and currency of library's discovery system and/or OPAC<br>• Usability and currency of library's service help pages and tools<br>• Provision and help with free research or collaboration tools such as citation managers and Google apps<br>• Provision and help with paid and free research and statistical programs such as OpenRefine, Tableau, and SPSS<br>• Events and space for online learners to meet and work together in person or virtually |

**Table 2.2   Service Inventory Template**

| Service Name | Current Name of the Service |
|---|---|
| Service definition | Very briefly, describe what the service is. This may be more controversial than it appears. It is possible that practitioners perceive the definition differently than service heads or library leaders. For the inventory, the practitioner definition is the most important. Gaps between the perceived service definitions are something to address in the final analysis. |
| Service lead | The person responsible for managing the service. |
| Service contact | Usually the service lead's contact information. This may be necessary for reviewers later in the process. |
| Service location | Where do users engage with this service? Probably a website address, LibGuide, phone number, etc. |
| Service availability | Times of the day, days of the week, days of the year. |
| Expected turnaround time | If the service includes requests or electronic responses (Document Delivery, Email Reference), what is the expected turnaround time to complete the transaction? Again, there may be discrepancies between different groups in the library. |
| Primary user group (intended) | What is the target user group of the service? Again, the user group as defined by the practitioner at this stage is the most critical to capture. Discrepancies or differences of opinion should be noted for later analysis. |
| Secondary user group (intended) | Possibly there is a secondary user group the library wants to reach with a service, but they are not the primary or priority group. |
| Unintended user groups (actual) | This column allows you to record groups that currently use a service that is not intended or geared for them. Perhaps community members are often referred to an alumni services page that doesn't pertain to them. |
| Supported programs/ initiatives | Indicate if the service specifically addresses programs or initiatives such as early childhood education, graduate engineering students, or English-language learners. |
| Current usage by intended users | If possible, report usage by primary or secondary user groups only. The organization should use the measure most relevant to them. Daily chat transactions, weekly reference-level transactions, monthly PDF downloads, unique webpage visitors by quarter, etc. |
| Base level service description | Very briefly describe in generic terms the baseline function of the service. Answer patron questions in real time. |

tool or method. Including as many employees as possible in the assessment will contribute to employee investment in the results as well as ensure the tool does not overlook important details.

## Analysis of Available Data

Before starting with the more interactive methods of a needs assessment, it is recommended to review what data the library already has available. This should include usage of electronic collections, resources, tutorials, and other digital learning objects. Your library may even collect what kind of users access these resources. Virtual chat and email numbers, along with any ratings or qualitative descriptions, should be collected. Hopefully, webpage views and the analytics associated with those views such as location, operating system, device, and time of day, week, month, and year are available to you. Analytics may also show you click paths throughout websites and LibGuides. Individual or groups of librarians may be collecting learning outcome achievement or student success data they are willing to share. Numbers of students taught in virtual instruction sessions or attending virtual workshops might exist, along with their disciplines and instructor names. Others might be keeping track of how many times patrons request a certain resource, service, product, or space that's not available. These data sets should inform what questions appear on surveys, themes needing to be addressed in focus groups, and potential populations and virtual spaces for observations. Knowing what data you have and what data you still need is also a critical gap to identify and address.

## Surveys and Feedback Activities

To target surveys to online users, embed them in resource portals, online learning websites or LibGuides, chat and help pages, tech help pages, remote access pages, and the learning management system (LMS). Ask online instructors and tutors to share the survey with students or patrons. Share a link to the survey whenever online help or reference is provided. Surveys can be made with free service like Survey Monkey or paid software applications like LibWizard (from SpringShare) or Qualtrics. Libraries can also ask users to perform card-sorting exercises for website and online portal designs, covered in greater depth in Chapter 3. Refer to the KSU Libraries' study presented above for some ideas on relevant survey questions for online users.

## Focus Groups

Focus groups allow more in-depth conversations to be had with small groups of users, providing reviewers more insight into themes suggested by surveys. Focus groups can assist in brainstorming new ideas or reasons for current issues. Focus groups are where individual stories are shared, which help reviewers build complete pictures of user personas and activities. The interaction of multiple participants can also be fruitful as people connected to the library in different ways discuss services and resources, how they use these things, and what they mean in their everyday lives and to their personal goals. Focus groups of mixed populations as well as more homogeneous ones (youth and teens, faculty, graduate students, library public service employees, seniors, etc.) should be constituted.

On-site and online focus groups should be held by trained facilitators. Higher education institutions and municipalities may have formal training on running focus groups. There are also many manuals and online guides to running focus groups. There's even a Coursera MOOC about it! The National Consortium of Interpreter Education Centers offers an excellent guide with tip sheets on the art of facilitating focus groups at their website: www.interpreter education.org. The results of the focus groups should be transcribed for analysis and dissemination. Summaries highlighting strengths, challenges, and suggestions as well as word clouds are useful ways to share focus group results.

### Observations

It's difficult to imagine how you would observe online learners during a needs assessment. Unlike a physical needs assessment observation, the reviewer cannot just fade into the background of a space and watch patrons interact with staff, each other, or move from A to B as they utilize the library. There are some helpful physical observations to be had, such as an internal department meeting or a curriculum planning meeting for an online course or program. You may try to observe the on-campus meeting of an online cohort or a class session of a hybrid section. However, most of the observation will be virtual and requires a little more effort on the part of the reviewer.

There are many virtual reference services that allow an observer or trainee to observe an interaction. This observation can be followed up with questions to the librarian and patron. Ask to sit in on online information literacy instruction sessions, workshops, and/or office hours. If your library does tutoring or mentoring online, try to join in the web conference or email thread to observe that communication. Reading transcripts of chat or email can also be a type of observation, even if it occurs after the fact.

### Understanding the Landscape

Maybe the most comfortable for library folks, understanding the landscape begins with a literature review. Identify three to five documents—articles, briefs, and example strategic plans—for the entire library to read. These documents should focus on best practices and future trends for your library type, providing your team members a baseline to work from. Additionally, the assessment team will want to read program reviews, strategic plans, and to broaden their knowledge base. Speaking to other libraries that have completed a needs assessment process or recently revamped online instruction or service programs will also be useful. This is the time in the process to forge contacts and allies that can advise on and review your process.

## Sharing the Results and Making the Plan

How you present this analysis to stakeholders, especially those needed to realize any changes and support them administratively, is often as important as identifying the gaps in the first place. An in-depth report is excellent for practitioners and disseminating within the professional literature. Shorter, more concise overviews may be more effective at the higher administrative levels. This would be more of an executive summary including a SWOT-type analysis. To help you understand what you're getting into, let's review some methods for sharing results.

There are multiple frameworks for organizing the results of your analysis. A needs assessment report will usually include:

- Introduction and background explaining why the study was done and who supported it.

- Methods describing how qualitative and quantitative data was collected, which were the strongest or weakest methods for gathering the data, and key participant included in the study.

- Key findings that summarize and analyze the data collected; for a needs assessment this will especially focus on the gaps in resources, services, perception, awareness, and satisfaction.

- Recommendations describing improvement or additions to resources and services, monetary or staff investments required to achieve these, and any further study or investigation that needs to be done.

A very traditional framework is a SWOT analysis, which looks at the strengths, weaknesses, opportunities, and threats identified from your work and creates an action plan to address or leverage them. But SWOT is not the only game in town when it comes to organizational analysis. Let's look at a few different frameworks that you could apply.

### SWOT (Strength, Weaknesses, Opportunities, Threats) Analysis

In a SWOT analysis, as shown in Figure 2.2, internal strengths and weaknesses and external opportunities and threat are listed on a matrix. These are based on your inventory and needs assessment, which together make up a type of environmental scan.

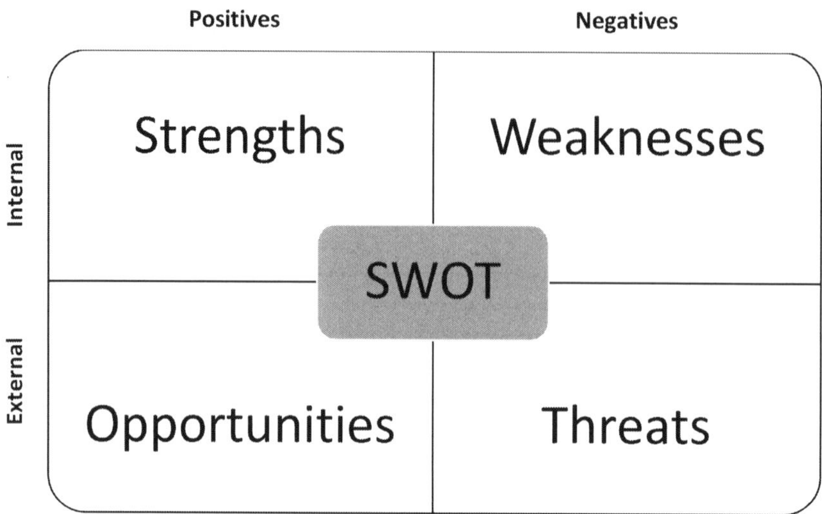


**Figure 2.2**   SWOT analysis.

*Strengths* and *weaknesses* are internal factors of the organization. They include:

- Human Resources: Staff and faculty, volunteers, administrators, student assistants, target populations.
- Physical Resources: Spaces, collections, equipment.
- Financial Resources: Budgets, grants, donors, fund-raising, endowments.
- Services, Programming, Activities: Services you provide to your organization, field, or profession, programs you run or participate in, activities your employees or organization engages in.
- Reputation and Experience: What is your organization known for? What knowledge or training does it have or need?

*Opportunities* and *threats* are external factors. They include:

- Future Trends: Preparedness for what's coming next, your relevancy.
- Funding and Resource Allocation: What is the future outlook of your funding sources, and how do you fit into that?
- Demographics: Current and future users, preparedness for changes in user populations.
- Physical Environment: Space allocation, renovation, maintenance, and upkeep.

- Social Environment: Future attitudes toward your organization, support within the community or parent institution, the impact of cultural and social changes.

This analysis assists the group to define strategic directions, address current issues, strengthen areas that require growth, choose areas where it should divest resources, and raise awareness regarding possible challenges in the future. It should highlight the gaps, describe what you already have to fill them, reveal the resources you still need, and help the organization understand what's coming in the near future for better planning.

## SOAR (Strengths, Opportunities, Aspirations, Results) Analysis

Figure 2.3 illustrates an alternative analysis methodology: SOAR. A SOAR analysis also places factors on a matrix, but it purposefully downplays the negative factors in preference of a positive, growth-centric view. It more easily applies to specific services or programming, which will likely be more comfortable for many reviewing their online services. A meeting about aspirations sounds like a lot more fun than a meeting about organizational threats. For SOAR, look at:

*Strengths:* What is the organization doing really well? Capabilities, accomplishments, assets?

*Opportunities:* What external factors could improve service, programming, and collections? What user needs are unmet?

*Aspirations:* What does your organization or program or team want to be known for? What does a premier level of online services look like?

*Results:* What are the measurable outcomes of your goals and aspirations? How would you know if you're achieving your aspirations?

**Figure 2.3**   SOAR analysis.

## SCORE (Strengths, Challenges, Options, Responses, and Effectiveness) Analysis

A third possible framework for your planning is SCORE. Like SOAR, SCORE is designed to consider the resulting actions and evaluate the results of your efforts. SCORE is not always shown in a cyclical formation, but this author believes the iterative process of assessing needs, enacting a plan, and evaluating the effectiveness of results is best represented this way, as shown in Figure 2.4.

Using a SCORE framework, the team will consider:

*Strengths:* Existing resources and capabilities, services currently offered, support available from others.

*Challenges:* Issues that need to be addressed internally and externally to meet current needs and potential future trends. What resources and skills are missing?

*Options:* Identifies options the organization has to fill gaps exposed by the needs assessment. Defines opportunities and risks considering what resources, skills, and capabilities are available.

*Responses:* Describes responses from users, employees, others in the organization, partners, and vendors. What will the return be for a particular option?

*Effectiveness:* Accounts for the potential outcome and response against the cost to the organization. Will an option be effective, reliable, and sustainable? Defines how those things will be measured.

## Next Steps

Whether you choose a SWOT, SOAR, or SCORE analysis, you will want to disseminate the results to your organization at all levels and make at least a summary of the results available to your users. The results of this work could easily be summarized into a two-, three-, or five-year action plan to improve online education support or transition into a segment of a larger strategic plan.

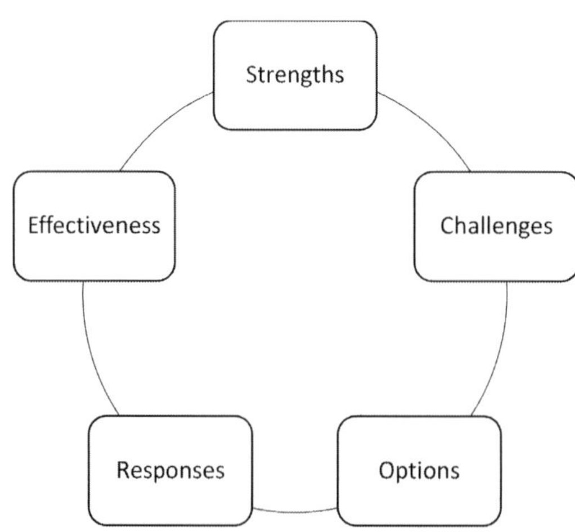


**Figure 2.4**   SCORE analysis.

## Conclusion

Evaluating your library's services to online learners through a needs assessment and service inventory is an important first step in understanding their needs, measuring your organization's ability to meet them, and identifying the critical gaps that currently exist. It's also an iterative process that puts the library in contact with multiple stakeholders and requires campus partners. Applying a diverse set of data collection methods such as surveys, focus groups, and observations will result in a more holistic view of your users and what they expect from the library. Using a SWOT, SOAR or SCORE analysis to explore and share the results will help the library set discrete goals and develop aspiration goals for improving or adding services, staff, and resources. Checking the effectiveness of your implemented responses is critical to the process and closes the loop with your users.

## References

Bonella, Laura, Joelle Pitts, and Jason Coleman. 2017. "How Do We Market to Distance Populations, and Does It Work? Results from a Longitudinal Study and a Survey of the Profession." *Journal of Library Administration* 57(1): 69–86.

Hebert, Andrea. 2016. "Hunting and Gathering: Attempting to Assess Services to Distance Learning Students." *Journal of Library & Information Services in Distance Learning* 10(3–4): 268–276.

Pitts, Joelle, Jason Coleman, and Laura Bonella. 2012. *We Built It, Why Didn't They Come? An Analysis of Library Awareness and Usage in the Kansas State University Distance Learning Community.* http://krex.ksu.edu.

Pitts, Joelle, Jason Coleman, and Laura Bonella. 2013. "Using Distance Patron Data to Improve Library Services and Cross-Campus Collaboration." *Internet Reference Services Quarterly* 18(1): 55–75.

# CHAPTER THREE

# Help Them Find What They Need: Making Resources Discoverable, Sharable, and Affordable

## Introduction

"Build it and they will come." It's a great quote, but librarians know you can build all you want, but learners will only come if they can find it and figure out how to access it. For those practicing online librarianship, the need to make resources for learning, teaching, research, and scholarship easily available to the broadest range of users with minimal library jargon or information literacy preparation is a necessity. As a core tenet of librarianship, information access is at the forefront of many library minds. There are innumerable methods, practices, and initiatives focused on increasing access to all knowledge. In this chapter, we focus on the most practical but also recently emerging efforts to improve information access for all users. This includes:

- Configuring search tools to provide the best, most accessible resources for all audiences and how to present them to users.

- Researching and adopting methods to open up library catalog data to more searchers, such as RDA, BIBFRAME, and Linked Open Data initiatives.

- High-quality Open Access (OA) and Open Educational Resource (OER) repositories to include in library catalogs, LibGuides, online courses, and library websites.

- Making OER for information literacy and supporting educators in incorporating OER into their courses.
- Tools library professionals can use to make good copyright and fair use decisions regarding the usage of library and open materials in a variety of formats.

## Configuring Search Tools for Access and Usability

Libraries and other information-serving organizations generally configure their searching tools to meet the needs of their most high-stakes users. This could include students, educators, scholars, community users, children, musicians, or any other specialized population. Although this design and configuration process may represent a collaborative, inclusive endeavor with representatives from across user groups, departments, and organizations, sometimes search interfaces that try to address committee input, advanced search methods, marketing and branding needs, and promotional expectations become cluttered, hard-to-navigate spaces that intimidate nonexperts. Unfortunately, many specialized library databases and even library search interfaces serve as complicated, overwrought examples of this process. To improve usability and accessibility, let's look at how these search interfaces came to be and what can be done to provide users the best search experience.

### Web-Scale Discovery Systems

Virtually all library users are familiar with the most ubiquitous search interface in the world: Google. A number of studies have found that students and new scholars prefer Google and Google Scholar over library catalogs and specialized database searching due to ease of use and familiarity (Du and Evans, 2011; Georgas, 2014). Google Scholar's development in 2004 spurred many library system vendors to build "discovery systems" that attempt to mimic Google's search style rather than the federated search methods previously tried. This is frequently referred to as web-scale discovery, a term used to describe a search method in which the patron uses a single entry point—a single search box—to retrieve results from many different publishers and platforms through full-text keyword searching of a pre-harvesed aggregate metadata index. This is in contrast to the traditional method of accessing multiple databases to search individual collections or indexes one at a time, utilizing complicated search strings or Boolean logic. These searches were often limited to just a few key fields in the library MARC record such as title, author, subject heading, and abstract rather than a full-text search of the content itself.

Library vendors' need to mimic the ease and scope of Google has spurred companies like ProQuest, Gale, and EBSCO to index content in a way that supports web-scale discovery. By sharing bibliographic data and indexes that include rich metadata and allowing discovery systems to search full text articles and eBooks, publishers and aggregators can improve discovery and retrieval of their resources. However, this sharing continues to be a sticking point as competing companies look to protect their intellectual property (IP), metadata, and bibliographic information rather than share it for optimal searching and display in a discovery system that may not be owned by them.

Web-scale discovery systems are considered easier to use by searchers because they take advantage of Google's familiar method of full-text keyword search and retrieving and ranking items based on algorithms. These algorithms take into account many factors for relevancy matching and result ranking, including:

- Exact phrase match on title, author, or subject heading.
- Keyword match in title.
- Keyword match in subject heading.
- Keyword match in abstract.
- Keyword match in author-supplied keywords.
- Frequency of matches in all fields and/or full text.
- Currency of publication date.
- Number of times cited by other works.
- Peer-reviewed status.
- Length of work.
- Material type.

Many discovery systems also provide facets for limiting search results, based on an Amazon-like user interface design. This is considered necessary because of the large number of results retrieved by full-text web-scale discovery. To sift through result sets frequently numbering in the hundreds of thousands or millions, users may want to limit by date, subject heading, material type, or publisher. Additionally, some discovery systems provide the ability to limit by peer-reviewed or open access status.

When participating in decision making regarding discovery system adoption, consider factors like open access facets, ability to locally customize relevancy, and if the vendor has access to the metadata of your most popular database or journal subscriptions. Options to customize or minimize interface components are also desirable so that you can locally configure your search interface to be as simple and user-friendly as possible. Institutions should at minimum allow all users to search their catalog or discovery system, especially public universities, colleges, and community colleges that need to provide community access to state or locally funded collections and resources. To promote the best level of access, do not require authentication for searching and make available an open access filter if at all possible, so that even nonaffiliated users can take advantage of the OER and OA content available from your discovery system.

## Google Scholar

Despite attempts to build web-scale discovery systems that match Google Scholar's ease of use, a 2011 study showed that of major repositories of government, university, and commercial scholarly citations available to U.S. researchers, including worldcat.org, nypl.org, library.yale.edu, and catalog .loc.gov, scholar.google.com (Google Scholar) was the most visited site—by over 200 percent more than the second leading site, sciencedirect.com (Calhoun, 2013, 148–149). And while they are an improvement on older federated searching options, discovery systems are often perceived as still more difficult to use than Google Scholar by many users (Oh and Colón-Aguirre, 2019). Considering this, it is recommended that libraries facilitate Google Scholar access and configuration to optimize connection to library-held or open access resources there.

### *Creating Customized Google Scholar Search Boxes*

At my university, Google Scholar is so popular with faculty and students that we have followed other libraries in adding Google Scholar as a search tab to our homepage, configured to offer our library resources through our link resolver. This tab bypasses the need for a user to set up their own Library Links setting in Google Scholar, which can be a barrier for users to gain access to your subscription content. To create a Google Scholar search that connects users directly to your subscriptions, preset the input form with your institution value. Here are the fairly simple steps required to build this form:

1.  Create a Google Scholar search form:

    ```
    <form id="googlesearch" method="get" action="https://scholar.google.com/
        scholar">
    <input name="as_sfid">
    <input type="submit" value="search">
    /form>
    ```

2.  Find your library's Google Scholar ID:

    (a)  Go to Google Scholar.

    (b)  Go to Settings.

    (c)  Click on Library Links.

(d)  Search your library.

(e)  In the Chrome browser, go to View > Developer > View Source.

(f)  Control + F to search for your institution name.

(g)  Find the value or id tag by your institution name; it will look something like id="gs_lib_15475584737496234600"

(h)  Add that value to your form input as <input type="hidden" name="inst" value="15475584737496234600">

3.  The final form will look like this:

```
<form id="googlesearch" method="get" action="https://scholar.google.com/
     scholar">

<input name="as_sfid">

<input type="hidden" name="inst" value="15475584737496234600">

<input type="submit" value="search">

/form>
```

4.  Link the form on your homepage.

At San Jose State University Library, that is done via a tab presented along with our other search forms. We have added helpful text under the search box so users know to click on our institution's link rather than the hyperlink for the article itself. Since its addition in 2018, the Google Scholar tab has become one of the most-used features on our homepage.

### *Efficacy of Google Scholar*

Recently, there has been some discussion in the library world that once Google Scholar reliably points to print resources it will be possible to drop expensive web-scale discovery systems altogether. Libraries contributing their print holdings to the OCLC WorldCat free union catalog can already encourage users to search for desired items at google.com with the addition of "find in library" (in quotations) or "add site:worldcatlibraries.org" (not in quotations) to their search terms. This will show the availability of print items in the user's local libraries through the WorldCat catalog.

Still, some debate remains about the comprehensive retrieval ability of Google Scholar among library and research folks. Some recent studies have shown that Google Scholar exhibits excellent, and in some cases perfect, performance in retrieval of seminal works, current scholarship, and gold-standard studies. A 2009 study of 29 systematic reviews in the major medical publications *Cochrane Library* and the *Journal of the American Medical Association* (*JAMA*) found that all 738 of the gold standard studies used in the reviews were retrieved through Google Scholar searches (Gehanno, Rollin, and Darmoni, 2013). In 2015 a comparison of library federated searches and

Google Scholar searches found that Google Scholar more easily led students to scholarly books and articles, although it should be said that the overall quality of the articles was found to be slightly higher from the federated library search (Georgas, 2015, 142–144).

Wilkes and Gurney found that even as far back as 2009, two-thirds of first-year students preferred using the Internet over library resources for research, and after two semesters there was a significant increase in comfort looking for research articles in Google Scholar with a minimal increase in comfort with library databases. Although students do want to limit to peer review and full text, the ease of searching in Google trumps the availability of these tools in the library databases (Wilkes and Gurney, 2009).

### *Google Scholar for Nonmatriculated Learners*

When supporting nonmatriculated individuals and to help users continue their scholarly pursuits after graduation, providing tips on how to access free or open content through Google Scholar can be very helpful. There is currently no way to limit to open access or un-paywalled content in the Google Scholar search interface. However, there are search strategies that support those unable to take advantage of library content from a distance. This includes looking for items that have a PDF, HTML, or DOC version available and checking the "All versions" link under the snippet to see more versions of items with no free content link. The other available versions may include open access conference proceedings related to the article or free preprints in an institutional repository.

## Other Discovery Tools

Peer-to-peer sharing at Researchgate.org, Academia.edu, Mendeley.com, or similar websites may also assist those engaging in research with limited access to scholarly resources. Here researchers can sign up, connect to others in their discipline, track citations of their work, and request a full-text copy of an article directly from an author. If the shared full-text document is used only for personal research, fair use guidelines arguably apply. We will look more at fair use later in the chapter.

Although not intended for the purpose of library access, the IPEDS College Map at nces.ed.gov/ipeds/CollegeMap will show users the nearest colleges and universities to their location. Public colleges and universities are often bound to provide community users access to their general print collections, which can be an invaluable resource to nonmatriculated online learners. Additionally, community users can often access electronic databases and journals once inside a university library. As we've already learned, by using search strategies in Google that limit to the WorldCat catalog, anyone may discover print materials in a nearby library. As more libraries jump on the BIBFRAME bandwagon and harness the power of linked data, Google searches will take users directly to local library holdings even without additional search qualifiers. Next, we'll explore how your library can begin to look into these new protocols and in what ways librarians serving online learners can advocate for their adoption.

## Linking the Library Catalog to the Semantic Web

If information wants to be free, why do libraries continue to use siloed catalog systems that describe holdings in a metadata format that is virtually unreadable by the Internet? For a group of people and organizations professionally obsessed with providing access to and promoting discovery of resources we should be relentlessly pushing a migration of library catalogs to a format that is easily indexed and integrated into the world's largest source of information, the World Wide Web. When a searcher types in "What is To Kill a Mockingbird about?" a link to the eBook, related scholarly articles, and documentaries available at local libraries should be highlighted in Google's "Knowledge Panel," regardless of where the patron is. The same should be true for any health topics, governmental policies and reports, and social issues.

Ensuring your materials, including items in your institutional repository, digital collections, and any added OER or OA materials, are cataloged using RDA (Resource Description and Access) and provided URIs is a good start. RDA supports the linked data principles laid out in RDF (Resource Description Framework), which are necessary for library records to be included in the semantic web. Let's briefly look at what that means.

## Linked Data

Linked data are the structured data elements across the web that are connected through HTTP URIs (Uniform Resource Identifiers). URIs are names (URNs) and locators (URLs) for things online. If we provide registered URIs for the items in our records and describe them using an RDF-compatible standard, in this case RDA, machines read that URI and the description we provided and link it with other data already online. This is linked data. The semantic web is that part of the World Wide Web structured by linked data into a standardized, machine-readable format that allows computers to create contextual connections between objects like records, data sets, webpages, images, etc., and then retrieve them dynamically during web searching.

There is a distinction to be made between linked data and linked open data, which is a term you may come across in the library and information architecture literature. Some data is available on the web using machine-readable metadata and standardized description and yet is not actually available for everyone to use—that is, linked data that is not open. Alternatively, open data can be shared on the web that does not provide adequate description in the standard format to allow it to be linked data, making it just open data. But when data that is available freely to everyone is also shared with a standardized description and URI, allowing it to be linked and made part of the semantic web, it is understood to be linked open data. There are multiple initiatives to support the widening of the linked open data cloud in order to build a more effective semantic web.

## RDA

Resource Description and Access (RDA) standard, initially released in 2010, is a package of data elements, guidelines, and instructions for describing physical and digital items. It was collaboratively developed by U.S., Canadian, and UK library associations in response to the need for a flexible metadata standard, compatible with user-focused linked-data applications and semantic searching. RDA provides more information about relationships between creator and work, which helps algorithms link records to queries through contextual connections. RDA is also designed to be end-user-friendly by replacing abbreviations, Latin terms, and bracketed information with natural, non-cataloger language. It allows for culturally appropriate terms (such as Qur'an rather than Koran) and provides more information on media type and player type so users know how to access desired items. A good starting point for those interested in RDA is the *RDA for the Non-Catalogers* webinar and slide set by the Association for Library Collections and Technical Services (ALCTS).

## BIBFRAME

Moving to BIBFRAME (Bibliographic Framework) from traditional MARC records is the next major step in connecting the library to the semantic web. The MARC record format silos library data because it is unreadable by any machine outside a library-specific system. Even archives and museums rarely use MARC, though we consider them closely related to libraries. The Library of Congress has been developing BIBFRAME since 2012 as a way to help libraries connect their records to the linked open data cloud (www.loc.gov /bibframe). Remember, linked data is what allows the semantic web and contextual connections to work. BIBFRAME is a data model that allows RDA library records to be connected to linked data elements through their joint adherence to RDF.

By using linked open data URIs in catalog records, we can expose our holdings in a meaningful way to the computers that perform searches and make connections across the web. This allows library content to be discovered and delivered through semantic queries in search engines like Google, Bing, and Duck Duck Go, which retrieve resources and information contextually related to a search and display it in dynamic, location-centric formats. Some integrated library systems (ILS), such as Ex Libris's Alma, provide built in support for MARC to BIBFRAME migration. An increasing number of larger libraries and library systems are successfully experimenting with BIBFRAME, including the San Francisco Public Library and Princeton University. RDA, URIs, and BIBFRAME allow all those open access English department theses in your institutional repository to be found and added to result lists when the end-user types in "What is to Kill a Mockingbird about?"

## Finding High-Quality Open Access and OER Materials

Table 3.1 provides just a few examples of the many high-quality Open Educational Resources (OER), Open Access (OA) textbooks, Digital Learning Object (DLO) repositories and Open Online Courseware that are appropriate for K–12, college, and adult level learning. These resources can take many forms from short videos, to virtual labs, to eTextbooks, to full online courses. Some, like the Project Gutenberg and OpenStax Textbook titles, are available for copy cataloging into your library's catalog. Some might be better suited for a website helping faculty find OER, such as a LibGuide with links to OER and OA resources by subject or discipline. These resources are in addition to directories and indexing that expose Open Access manuscripts (Directory of Open Access Book, or DOAB) and journals (Directory of Open Access Journals, or DOAJ) that can be added to your library eResources or mined by individuals for publishing options. Table 3.1 lists just a few of the most notable resources in major subject areas.

Any librarian working in the online learning space should be aware of the breadth of options available and understand the main ways faculty and students interact with these resources. Downloading PDFs, embedding virtual interactive labs, adopting and expanding on OA textbooks, adapting open courseware modules in an LMS—there are many ways this content is used, remixed, and shared. An understanding of copyright, fair use, Creative Commons licensing, and how works enter and act in the public domain is extremely helpful. It's also useful to know how to create and support the creation of OER and OA content. In the next sections we'll explore tools for making this type of content and resources for interpreting and applying open licenses.

**Table 3.1   Recommended Open Access and OER Resources by Subject**

| Subject/Discipline | Resource |
|---|---|
| Art and design | *Khan Academy* is famous for its math and science video tutorials, but this site also has a large history repository, including a SmartHistory introduction to art history prepared by a former SUNY Dean of Graduate Studies and the Fashions Institute of Technology (www.khanacademy.org/humanities).<br><br>*AICT (Art Images for College Teaching)* from the University of Michigan is a repository where educators share royalty-free images that may be useful in college courses (quod.lib.umich.edu/a/aict).<br><br>*MetPublications* offers five decades of publications on art history available for free download (metmuseum.org/art/metpublications).<br><br>*The National Gallery of Art* provides OER teaching packets for K–12 educators, hosts downloadable high-resolution images, and offers free online courses for integrating art into your online curriculum (www.nga.gov/education.html). |
| Business/accounting/finance | *Open Textbook Library*—Business and accounting & finance are well covered in this OA textbook repository from the University of Minnesota (open.umn.edu/opentextbooks).<br><br>*GlobalEDGE* shares a wealth of knowledge on international business practices and export rules offered by Michigan State University's International Business Center (globaledge.msu.edu/reference-desk). |
| Communication/journalism | *Saylor.org* offers thousands of high-quality open courses online across a variety of topics, including communication (learn.saylor.org/course).<br><br>*MIT Open Courseware* is a MOOC platform with some of the best open online courses and OER available today. The MIT Media Arts and Sciences department has made good use of the platform, providing a variety of OER in the discipline (ocw.mit.edu/courses/media-arts-and-sciences). |
| Education | *OpenLearn*—Education and development is just part of this UK "Open University" MOOC platform that can be used in whole or part as OER for online courses (www.open.edu/openlearn/education). |

(continued)

**Table 3.1** *(continued)*

| Subject/Discipline | Resource |
|---|---|
| | *Edutopia* is a growing repository of free teaching resources from the George Lucas Educational Foundation (www.edutopia.org/topics). |
| | *PBS Learning Media* offers thousands of videos and DLOs gathered by the Public Broadcasting Company, ranked by grade level and made available for reuse (www.pbslearningmedia.org). |
| | *UMASS Boston OpenCourseWare* provides quality open courseware on early childhood education development, along with many other areas of study (ocw.umb.edu). |
| Engineering/ programming | *MIT OpenCourseWare* is an excellent place to find seminal open courses on all kinds of engineering topics (ocw.mit.edu). |
| | *Codecademy* offers free classes in twelve programming languages (www.codecademy.com). |
| | *InTech* hosts nearly 800 open access textbooks on engineering topics by highly cited, well-respected authors (intechopen.com/books/subject/engineering). |
| | *Engineertech.org* offers free engineering simulations online covering fundamental engineering concepts such as thermodynamics, circuits, and lean manufacturing. |
| English/literature | *Project Gutenberg* is one of the most famous repositories of digitized text in the public domain. Gutenberg Project MARC records can also be added to your library catalog (www.gutenberg.org). |
| | *HathiTrust* is another well-known digitized book repository created by the best research libraries in the country. Records can be downloaded to your local catalog or often come available from electronic index subscriptions (www.hathitrust.org). |
| Information technology/ cybersecurity | *BookBoon* provides free PDF access to thousands of OA books, including over 150 on IT and programming topics (bookboon.com/en/it-programming-ebooks). |
| K–12 curriculum | *OpenEd* is a leading OER repository for K–12 that matches videos, games, and assessments to Common Core learning objectives. Content can be embedded in nearly any online learning platform (about.opened .com). |

*(continued)*

**Table 3.1**   (*continued*)

| Subject/Discipline | Resource |
| --- | --- |
|  | *Curriki* is a global platform for discovering and sharing customizable lesson plans and activities for K–12 education (www.curriki.org).<br><br>*NYEngage* offers Common Core aligned curricular content for English and Math supported by the New York State Education Department (www.engageny.org). |
| Languages | *MERLOT* is an OER repository that provides peer review features to help educators assess and select OER content. While it covers virtually all subjects, it also hosts content in a wide variety of languages (www.merlot.org). |
| Mathematics | *OpenStax Textbooks* publishes high-quality OA textbooks from prealgebra to college physics, along with textbooks applicable to many introductory college courses. They can be downloaded or viewed online. WorldCat records are available for copy cataloging (cnx.org).<br><br>*The Orange Grove* is Florida's OA/OER digital repository. It hosts DLOs, open courseware, OA textbooks, and much more on a wide variety of topics. Orange Grove's math and science sections are particularly strong and offer many full digital OA textbooks (www.floridashines.org/orange-grove).<br><br>*Open Textbook SUNY* is an OA textbook repository allowing free online access or PDF download of works on many topics, especially mathematics, logic, engineering, and programming (textbooks.opensuny.org). |
| Physical science | *University of California, Irvine,* has an excellent array of OA physical science courses (ocw.uci.edu/courses).<br><br>*Astronomy Image Explorer* hosts hundreds of thousands of astronomy and astrophysics images from peer-reviewed journals, searchable and sortable in one database (www.astroexplorer.org).<br><br>*National Academies of Science, Engineering and Medicine* publishes over 200 well-researched books a year that inform national and global policy. Most are available for free digital download (www.nap.edu). |

(continued)

**Table 3.1**  (*continued*)

| Subject/Discipline | Resource |
|---|---|
|  | *LibreTexts Project* offers free OA textbooks on a variety of subjects. Most impressive is their Chem TextMaps project, which works to map interactive OER and OA texts to existing popular chemistry textbooks so instructors don't have to (chem.libretexts.org). |
| Social sciences | *Films for Action* is a "community-powered library" providing access to over 4,500 free films relevant to social action and justice (www.filmsforaction.org). |
|  | *Academic Earth* is an aggregator of free online courses. This site leads users to various free MOOC and online course platforms based on subject. Their sociology list is particularly robust (academicearth.org/sociology). |
|  | *National Academies Press* is a policy research press. Industry and labor are well covered by this publisher, which allows free digital downloads of 444 eBooks on related topics (www.nap.edu/topic/289/industry-and-labor). |
|  | *Carnegie Melon's Open Learning Initiative (OLI)* offers introductory free online courses on many topics, including psychology, logic, and languages (oli.cmu.edu). |
| Virtual labs | *Texas A&M Virtual Math Lab* provides interactive experience without a physical classroom using online DLOs (www.wtamu.edu/academic/anns/mps/math/mathlab). |
|  | *ChemCollectives Virtual Chem Labs* provides users the opportunity to explore a virtual chemistry bench and all the fun things that can happen there with interactive DLOs (www.chemcollective.org/vlab/vlab.php). |
|  | *HHMI's (Howard Hughes Medical Institute) Biointeractive* hosts thousands of activity-based DLOs for biology, including virtual labs (www.hhmi.org/biointeractive/explore-virtual-labs). |

## Creating and Sharing OER and Reusable Course Content

Although libraries frequently struggle with sharing their holdings information with each other and the wider web, they have a long history of freely sharing metadata, cataloging information, toolkits, information literacy videos, instructional content, and data. The concepts of sharing, reusing, collecting, remixing, and fair use make sense to library people. It's not surprising then that so many emerging initiatives in higher education about lowering course costs through the creation of free reusable content and OA textbooks are run from the library. It is there that a dedication to the open access mission and an expertise regarding content usage and creator rights converge.

## Library Contributions to OA/OER Initiatives

SPARC, the Scholarly Publishing and Academic Resource Coalition, hosts a directory of OER activity on their site at sparcopen.org/our-work/connect-oer. The majority of projects are housed in the libraries of higher education organizations. These projects range from large, well-funded initiatives and repositories at research institutions to smaller efforts such as websites and minigrants from state and community colleges. Some notable examples are:

- Temple University Libraries' Alternative Textbook Project supporting and funding faculty to expand use of OER.
- Oregon State University (OSU) Libraries partnered with OSU Press and OSU Extended Campus to create an open textbook publishing initiative.
- Texas A&M Libraries hosted a two-day OER workshop for all SEC institutions.
- California State University Libraries' Affordable Learning Solutions initiatives seeks to lower education cost by replacing textbooks with OER and OA texts in large GE courses.

Many of these projects start with librarian-to-faculty outreach, proposing library resources or OA textbooks as alternatives to expensive course materials. This can be as simple as matching course textbooks with library multiuser eBooks or OA textbooks. Faculty can share the eBook link on their course syllabus, or the library can publish an online list for students to access directly.

Librarians may also support faculty by suggesting OER, government resources, or content that the library owns or subscribes to that can be put together in PDF readers or online reading lists to replace textbooks. Librarians supporting MOOCs should be especially vigilant in identifying OA textbooks and OER content as an alternative to paid content, as so many nontraditional students with varying economic means tend to populate MOOCs. I recently discovered that librarians at San Francisco State University were coauthoring OA textbooks with faculty as part of their work on affordability. This not only contributes to the availability of OA educational content but also contributes to librarians' own work as scholars and their professional reputation.

## School Librarians as OER Curators

School librarians have become an important force in the OER movement over the last decade as they seek out supporting materials for new curriculum standards that are affordable and easily accessible to all teachers and students. School librarians curate collections aligned with Common Core, educate teachers on evaluating OER, and review OER for inclusion in repositories such as OERCommons. OpenEd, Curriki, Gooru, and PBS Learning Media are all excellent K–12 OER repositories and are largely supported by educators and librarians in the field. In 2019, the American Association of School Librarians released a toolkit to facilitate school librarian efforts to create and curate OER. The toolkit is free for download at www.ala.org/aasl /toolkits.

ISKME (Institute for the Study of Knowledge Management in Education) in partnership with Florida State University School of Information is currently engaged in a study of OER and school librarians. Early findings published in the spring of 2019 indicate that states, districts, and school librarian degree programs should make OER curation a formal part of the school librarian role; encourage school librarian collaborations around OER programs; and extend these librarians' knowledge of open licensing (Jimes, 2019). ISKME's draft report is available under the title *The Role of School Librarians in OER Curation: A Framework to Guide Practice* (ISKME, 2019).

## Digital Library Initiatives

While academic libraries focus on OA initiatives and institutional repositories to host open content and school librarians work to curate OER collections supporting Common Core, the Digital Public Library of America (DPLA) has undertaken the incredibly ambitious and important initiative of creating one search portal for all of America's publicly available digital collections from American libraries, archives, museums, and other cultural heritage organizations. To do this the DPLA aggregates metadata and thumbnails for millions of items and makes them discoverable through their website. This metadata often includes URIs so that DPLA data can be enriched by linked open data. Those URIs also promote the retrieval of local content aggregated in the DPLA during semantic web search, increasing the discoverability of many local collections. Through the DPLA, scholars, instructors, and learners can find images, primary texts, videos, oral histories, and maps for research, assignments, course content, and lifelong learning. Many items in the DPLA are in the public domain, but copyright status varies by item.

The DPLA also offers a large suite of APIs that developers can use to build applications; digital humanities scholars access to analyze large data and image sets; and researchers in urban planning, ethnic studies, and geographic information systems take advantage of for land-use, gentrification, and map studies. Public libraries interested in participating in the DPLA should contact their local Service Hub for information and resources. Helpful information can be found at pro.dp.la/hubs.

The DPLA is just one example of large digital collection projects supported by public libraries. The Chicago Collections Consortium is a collaboration between the Chicago Public Library, the Art Institute of Chicago, and other local museums and universities that works to preserve Chicago culture and history through a consortia digital collection. The Mountain West Digital Library and Boston Library Consortium are other examples. Europeana Collections serves a similar function for Europe, providing access to over fifty-eight million items from European museums, galleries, libraries, and archives.

## Supporting OER Creation

Librarians supporting online instruction and learning or content creation should be especially familiar with a variety of digital tools that support the creation and sharing of digital OER. This will allow you to advocate for the use of free and reusable materials in online or hybrid courses and help ensure content access for all potential users. Keeping current on screencasting and digital publication tools, resources for creating digital learning objects such as OER Commons, and free application builders for mobile learning are crucial to supporting online educators and to help the library create virtual content. A wide variety of digital creation and collaboration tools are described in Chapter 7.

## Understanding Copyright, Fair Use, and Creative Commons

As a library professional supporting online education, it is likely you will need to interpret copyright restrictions and fair use guidelines for yourself and consult with others as they prepare course materials. This next section provides tools for understanding copyright and making fair use determinations. It also offers insight into Creative Commons licensing to assist in interpretation of reuse rules or in licensing your own content.

### Understanding Copyright

According to the U.S. Copyright Office, copyright is a form of protection provided by the laws of the United States (Title 17, U.S. Code) to the authors of "original works of authorship," including literary, dramatic, musical, artistic, and certain other intellectual works (U.S. Copyright Office, 2017). This protection is available to both published and unpublished works. Section 106 of the 1976 Copyright Act generally gives the owner of copyright the exclusive right to do, and to authorize others to do, the following (U.S. Copyright Office, 2016):

- Reproduce the work in copies or phonorecords.
- Prepare derivative works based on the work.
- Distribute copies or phonorecords of the work to the public by sale or other transfer of ownership, or by rental, lease, or lending.
- Perform the work publicly, in the case of literary, musical, dramatic, and choreographic works, pantomimes, and motion pictures and other audiovisual works.
- Display the work publicly, in the case of literary, musical, dramatic, and choreographic works, pantomimes, and pictorial, graphic, or sculptural works, including the individual images of a motion picture or other audiovisual work.
- Perform the work publicly by means of a digital audio transmission.

## Exceptions for Academic Institutions

The Copyright Act contains some specific exceptions for the use of copyright-protected materials by academic institutions. These provisions include (U.S. Copyright Office, 2016):

- Section 107 on fair use, which applies to activities such as the use of excerpts for illustration or comment; the unexpected and spontaneous reproduction of classroom materials; and the creation of parodies.
- Section 108 on reproduction by libraries and archives, which applies to activities such as archiving; replacing lost, damaged, or obsolete copies; patron requests for entire works; and interlibrary loans.
- Section 109 on first sale, which permits the resale or lending of copies of works, providing the basis for library lending and the sale of used books.
- Section 110 on the use of materials in an educational setting, which permits certain types of content use in the classroom and in distance education.

Be aware that articles received through interlibrary loan from another library are licensed for single use only. This means they cannot legally be duplicated or posted online.

## Understanding Fair Use

Two documents that educators and librarians will find helpful when inter-preting fair use guidelines are the U.S. Copyright Office's 2017 Circular 21 *Reproduction of Copyrighted Works by Educators and Librarians* and the U.S. Patent and Trademark Office's 1998 Report *Conference on Fair Use: Final Report to the Commissioner on the Conclusion of the Conference on Fair Use.* The suggestions below are based on generally accepted interpretations of these guidelines. Fair use is not a codified law, but rather a defense against a claim of copyright infringement. As such, these recommendations are a starting point for your own research and interpretation. Whenever in doubt, it is advisable to seek the council of a legal professional.

When determining if the use of a copyrighted work falls under fair use, there are four factors to consider according to existing legal guidance. These are purpose of the use, nature of the use, the amount of the work that will be used, and the effect of the use to the potential market of the work. Table 3.2 provides an overview of things to consider related to each factor and if it favors or opposes fair use.

Figure 3.1 shows an example of using these factors to decide if a typical library service, course eReserves, falls under fair use. Please note that every institution should set its own guidelines and decide how much guidance they will provide to those making fair use determinations.

Once you determine that fair use applies, you will want to follow the existing standards for how much of a work is allowed to be utilized under fair use. Guidelines for portions of lawfully acquired copyrighted works that can be used according to fair use as indicated by the U.S. Copyright Office and U.S. Patent and Trademark Office reports noted above are shown in Table 3.3.

### *Creative Commons Licensing*

Creative Commons is a nonprofit agency founded in 2001 to expand the range of works within the public domain, available for use and reuse at no cost, for intellectual, artistic, and entertainment purposes. This was princi-pally in reaction to U.S. copyright laws that many in the education, arts, and nonprofit sectors have found to be increasingly restrictive and punitive due to the successful lobbying efforts of large, wealthy media corporations look-ing to maintain their very profitable copyrights on famous works. The com-plicated and interesting history of copyright law can be found elsewhere, and I encourage you to learn more about it since it so deeply effects the mission of libraries. Nevertheless, by allowing creators to take control of their own rights, Creative Commons seeks to prevent the whole of our cultural output

**Table 3.2    The Four Factors of Fair Use**

| Favors Fair Use | Opposes Fair Use |
| --- | --- |
| **Purpose** | |
| The use is:<br>• For classroom/scholarly/research purposes<br>• Nonprofit<br>• For criticism/comment/parody<br>• Transformative | The use is:<br>• Commercial or for-profit<br>• For entertainment purposes<br>• Does not credit the creator |
| **Nature** | |
| The work is:<br>• Published<br>• Factual/nonfiction/fiction<br>• Important to an educational objective | The work is:<br>• Unpublished<br>• Creative/artistic<br>• Fictional |
| **Amount** | |
| The use:<br>• Involves a small quantity of the overall work<br>• Portion used is not central to the entire work | The use:<br>• Involves a large portion of the work or the entire work<br>• Involves the most significant portion of the work |
| **Effect** | |
| The use:<br>• Required the user to purchase original copy of work<br>• Requires one or few copies to be made<br>• Has no significant effect on the market for the work<br>• Is due to no similar product available on the market, such as when no individual electronic chapter of the book is available for purchase<br>• Is provided with restricted access, such as only to students in a particular course for the duration of that course | The use:<br>• Could replace sale of the work<br>• Requires numerous copies be made<br>• Impairs market potential of the work or derivatives<br>• Involves a portion of the work that could easily be purchased, such as an available electronic book chapter<br>• Involves posting the work to the open web<br>• Is repeated or long term |

Based on U.S. Copyright Office's 2017 Circular 21 *Reproduction of Copyrighted Works by Educators and Librarians* and the U.S. Patent and Trademark Office's 1998 Report *Conference on Fair Use: Final Report to the Commissioner on the Conclusion of the Conference on Fair Use.*

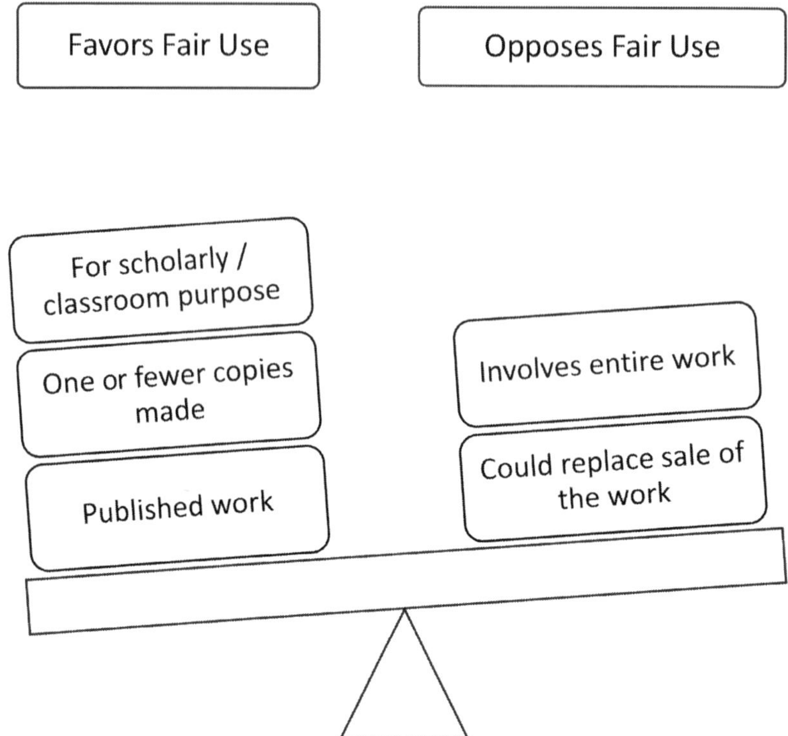


**Figure 3.1**  Weighing fair use factors for course reserves.

**Table 3.3  Fair Use Amounts for Various Media**

| Media | Amount Suggested to Meet Fair Use |
|---|---|
| Video | Up to 10% or 3 minutes, whichever is less |
| Text | Up to 10% or 1,000 words, whichever is less; one chapter out of a ten-chapter book |
| Music/lyrics/ music video | Up to 10%, but no more than 30 seconds |
| Illustrations/ photographs/ images | No more than five images from a single artist; 10% of a published collective work, but no more than fifteen works |
| Data sets | Up to 10% or 2,500 fields, whichever is less |

Based on U.S. Copyright Office's 2017 Circular 21 *Reproduction of Copyrighted Works by Educators and Librarians* and the U.S. Patent and Trademark Office's 1998 Report *Conference on Fair Use: Final Report to the Commissioner on the Conclusion of the Conference on Fair Use.*

from falling under ever-lengthening copyright laws that deny individuals the right to build on or remix existing cultural content.

To do this, Creative Commons offers a suite of licenses, known as CC license, that any creator can generate from the Creative Commons website at creativecommons.org. Creators apply CC licenses to their work, making it reusable to various degrees and with specific restrictions, depending on the way the creator wants to control the use of their content. Most OER and some OA content falls under a creator-generated CC license. To create, recommend, use, or remix this content you will need to become familiar with CC licenses and understand how to apply them in various scenarios.

In addition to the Creative Commons licenses that we will look at closely in this section, Creative Commons also supports legal advocacy and education around U.S. and global copyright and open access issues. This includes offering a Creative Commons Certification for Educators and Librarians. I had the privilege of beta-testing this online certificate course in 2018 and found it an engaging, informative course with well-planned assignments that resulted in shareable, instructive content perfect for social media or websites. For more information, go to www.certificates.creativecommons.org.

*Components and Icons.* CC licenses are created through a combination of discrete components that set requirements or limits on reuse and remixing of the work. Table 3.4 shows the icons for these components and describes their meaning.

*Licenses.* Creators put these license components together in various ways to create one of six CC licenses that can be applied to a work (seven if we count CC Zero, which creators use to relinquish their copyright). The currently available CC licenses listed from most open to least open can be seen in Table 3.5. To create a license for your own work, go to www.creative commons.org/choose and fill out a brief set of questions about how you want others to use your work. Creative Commons will generate a license for you that can be embedded in web content or saved as an image file and added to your work.

### Resources for Learning More

There are many resources for learning about copyright in the United States and abroad. The main U.S. government website for copyright, www.copyright.gov, provides resources for registering copyright and reviewing copyright law and federal regulation. From their homepage access the Fair Use Index to search fair use case law to help yourself and others make fair use decisions.

The Library Copyright Alliance (www.librarycopyrightalliance.org) lays out clearly the philosophy held by library professional organizations regarding

**Table 3.4   Creative Commons Icons and Their Meanings (2019)**

| License Name | Icon | Description |
| --- | --- | --- |
| CC: Creative Commons | | The Creative Commons logo indicates the item is licensed by the nonprofit organization Creative Commons. It precedes every Creative Commons. |
| BY: Attribution | | The BY icon represents attribution. BY requires that you give credit to the creator. Add this component to your license to allow others to copy, display, perform, remix, or build on your work if they attribute it to you. |
| SA: Share Alike | | The SA icon represents Share Alike. This requires that any future use of a work must be published with a license identical to that work. Add this component to your license if you want every use, remix, expansion, or derivative of your work to have an identical license to the one you've chosen. |
| ND: No Derivatives | | The ND icons represents No Derivatives. This means you can only use the work as is, verbatim. The work cannot be changed, expanded, or remixed in any way. Use No Derivatives when you want others to use your work exactly as it is, without any changes or additions. |
| NC: Noncommercial | | The NC icon represents Noncommercial. This icon allows you to copy, display, perform, remix, or build on the work in any way that is noncommercial (unless you have also chosen No Derivatives). Add this component to prevent commercial use of any work you are sharing with a CC license. |
| CC Zero | | The CC Zero icon represents the declaration: "No Right Reserved." Creators that use this license are putting no restrictions on the use of work and require no attribution. Although it's rarely legally possible to enter your own work into the public domain before the legal copyright limit is up, use CC Zero to effectively release the work from all copyright restriction immediately. |

*(continued)*

**Table 3.4** (*continued*)

| License Name | Icon | Description |
| --- | --- | --- |
| Public Domain | 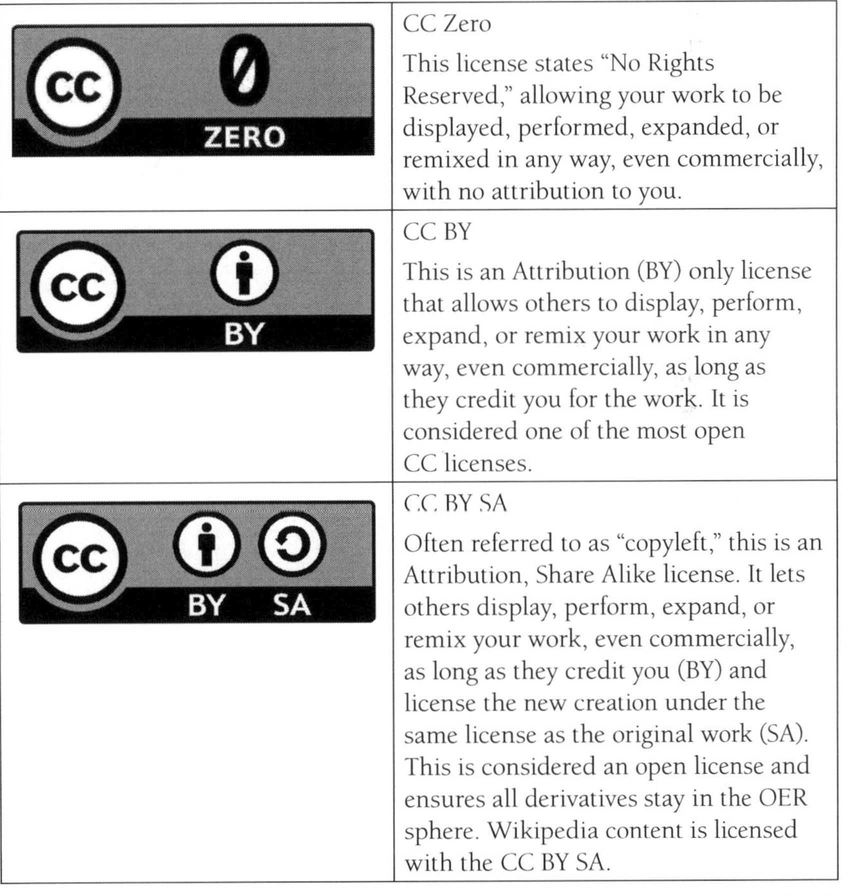 | This is the public domain icon. As noted, public domain is a legal status that works enter after a certain period of time. Although creators themselves can rarely legally release a work into the public domain, you may occasionally see a work reposted online that is already in the public domain and marked with this icon. |

**Table 3.5  Creative Commons Licenses (2019)**

| Icon | Description |
| --- | --- |
| | CC Zero<br><br>This license states "No Rights Reserved," allowing your work to be displayed, performed, expanded, or remixed in any way, even commercially, with no attribution to you. |
| | CC BY<br><br>This is an Attribution (BY) only license that allows others to display, perform, expand, or remix your work in any way, even commercially, as long as they credit you for the work. It is considered one of the most open CC licenses. |
| | CC BY SA<br><br>Often referred to as "copyleft," this is an Attribution, Share Alike license. It lets others display, perform, expand, or remix your work, even commercially, as long as they credit you (BY) and license the new creation under the same license as the original work (SA). This is considered an open license and ensures all derivatives stay in the OER sphere. Wikipedia content is licensed with the CC BY SA. |

(*continued*)

**Table 3.5**  (*continued*)

| | |
|---|---|
|  | CC BY NC<br><br>This is an Attribution, Noncommercial license. This license allows others to display, perform, expand, or remix your work, but only for noncommercial (NC) purposes, and they must credit you for the work (BY). However, they do not have to license the work under the same license as the original. |
|  | CC BY ND<br><br>This Attribution, No Derivative license allows others to display, share, or perform your work but allows no derivatives (ND) of the work. It must be reused in whole and without changes, and it must be attributed to you (BY). |
|  | CC BY NC SA<br><br>This license allows others to display, perform, expand, or remix your work but only for noncommercial (NC) use; they must credit you for the work (BY), and the new creation must be licensed under the same license as the original (SA). |
|  | CC BY NC ND<br><br>This is the Attribution, Noncommercial, No Derivative license. This license allows others to display, share, or perform your work if they credit you (BY) but only for noncommercial purposes (NC), and they may not change it in any way (ND). This is the most restrictive CC license available. Academic authors and researchers wishing to share their work with colleagues or students but protect their intellectual property and future market might use this license. |

copyright and fair use. This is an excellent resource for use in drafting library policies, philosophy statements, and advocacy documents.

There are also many well-made university and academic library sites that work to clarify copyright and fair use laws and help you work through the decision-making steps on when to use content and how. Before utilizing any online tools to make copyright and fair use decisions or recommendations, ensure it is current, cites legitimate legal or policy sources, takes a measured view on the issue, and comes from a well-respected organization or institution. Some suggested sites are:

- Fordham University Libraries Copyright Resources (fordham.libguides.com /copyright)

- Kent State University Libraries Copyright Resources (libguides.library.kent .edu/copyright)

- Stanford University Copyright and Fair Use, Charts and Tools Page (fairuse .stanford.edu/charts-and-tools)

## Conclusion

Supporting online learners in any type of library means ensuring they have the tools they need to easily discover and access high-quality resources. This can be done by configuring your search tools with users in mind, linking your library data to the larger web, and advocating for the use of OER and OA content that is freely available to everyone. Supporting faculty interested in creating open content and a comprehensive understanding of copyright, fair use, and Creative Commons licenses will be useful in evaluating open content and supporting educators in the adoption of these materials. There are many online resources to support this activity that you can adapt for use in your own organization.

## References

Calhoun, Karen. 2013. "Supporting Digital Scholarship: Bibliographic Control, Library Co-Operatives and Open Access Repositories." In *Catalogue 2.0: The Future of the Library Catalogue*, ed. Sally Chambers, 143–178. London: Facet Publishing.

Du, Jia Tina, and Nina Evans. 2011. "Academic Users' Information Searching on Research Topics: Characteristics of Research Tasks and Search Strategies." *The Journal of Academic Librarianship* 37(4): 299–306.

Gehanno, Jean-François, Laetitia Rollin, and Stefan Darmoni. 2013. "Is the Coverage of Google Scholar Enough to Be Used Alone for Systematic Reviews." *BMC Medical Informatics and Decision Making* 13(7).

Georgas, Helen. 2014. "Google vs. the Library (Part II): Student Search Patterns and Behaviors When Using Google and a Federated Search Tool." *portal: Libraries and the Academy* 14(4): 503–532.

Georgas, Helen. 2015. "Google vs. the Library (Part III): Assessing the Quality of Sources Found by Undergraduates." *portal: Libraries and the Academy* 15(1): 133–161.

Institute for the Study of Knowledge Management in Education (ISKME). 2019. *School Librarians as OER Curators: A Framework to Guide Practice.* https://docs.google.com/document/d/1wTzE7rKg9Kbzm3t24TIxIJy_bEA81sDqVvwlXPC7OYA/edit.

Jimes, Cynthia. 2019. *Changing Practice: School Librarians as OER Curators.* Institute for the Study of Knowledge Management in Education. https://www.iskme.org/our-ideas/changing-practice-school-librarians-oer-curators-0.

Oh, Kyong, and Mónica Colón-Aguirre. 2019. "A Comparative Study of Perceptions and Use of Google Scholar and Academic Library Discovery Systems." *College & Research Libraries* 80(6).

United States Copyright Office. 2016. *Copyright Laws of the United States and Related Laws Contained in Title 17 of the United States Code.* Circular 92. https://www.copyright.gov/title17/title17.pdf.

United States Copyright Office. 2017. *Copyright Basics.* Circular 1. https://www.copyright.gov/circs/circ01.pdf.

Wilkes, Janelle, and Lisa J. Gurney. 2009. "Perceptions and Applications of Information Literacy by First Year Applied Science Students." *Australian Academic & Research Libraries* 40(3): 159–171.

# PART 2

# Creating Community

# CHAPTER FOUR

# Help Them Help Each Other: Facilitating Peer Interactions and Creating Online Learning Communities

## Introduction

"Peer-to-peer learning offers a 'safe harbor' in which students can manage their own learning experiences by exploring, practicing and questioning . . . untethered from the hierarchy inherent in formal instruction environments or in working with professional librarians and staff."

—O'Kelly et al., 2015, 163

Peer learning has long been a staple in the educators' toolkit. Beginning with John Dewey's development of the constructivist learning theory in the early twentieth century, experimentation and research have proven the concept that students learn more deeply and retain information better through active, collaborative experiences rather than rote memorization. Recent work in social learning theory, presented originally by Albert Bandura in the 1960s and 1970s and built on by later researchers and practitioners, has shown that learners gain understanding and skill by observing others, deciding the effects of their observed behavior are positive, and subsequently modeling that behavior. In this way all learning is potentially a social dialogue, external and internal.

The sustained success of these learning theories tells us that requiring a learner to discuss, explain, model, observe, and debate concepts and processes with peers encourages critical thinking and analysis. It also improves retention and enhances the students' own perception of mastery. The flat power structure of the peer learning relationship relieves anxiety and provides the learner space to make mistakes and work out concepts with less scrutiny or pressure.

In the last decade or so the rise of online peer-to-peer instruction platforms has shown that these methods are valuable and effective even outside structured learning experiences and particularly in an online environment. According to YouTube, two billion users visit the site each month, many looking for someone like themselves to teach them how to apply makeup, build a robot, create an Excel formula, or roll fondant on a cake (Wojcicki, 2020). YouTube expertise is frequently determined only by the number of hits on a video and positive comments regarding the outcomes of a tutorial. That is, expertise is determined through peer evaluation of the content. The streaming platform Twitch is almost entirely dedicated to the sharing of live video game play, as entertainment and as real-time peer-to-peer tutorials on passing levels and gaining resources in various game titles. Quora and Yahoo Answers are platforms built for and dedicated to peer question-and-answer threads, while Yelp and Rotten Tomatoes leverage the trust people have in peers to rate and review consumer and entertainment experiences. Organizations dedicated entirely to peer learning have also emerged, such as SkillShare and the librarian-founded Peer 2 Peer University, or P2PU.

Peer-to-peer (P2P) learning comes in a myriad of modalities. Three of the most prevalent are peer tutoring, peer teaching, and peer mentoring. These modes designate an "expert" that imparts knowledge or experience to another learner through regulated interactions. Peer-assisted learning (PAL) methods describe both structured activities in which equal peer pairs provide feedback and coaching or in which a slightly more advanced student facilitates learning in a near-peer group. Peer learning communities are built through careful facilitation in course groups or cohorts. In addition to these more formal relationships, peer learning also encompasses educators' work to encourage peer interactions that enrich and enhance learning experiences online and on-campus.

P2P learning is important in all learning environments, but analysis of P2P contribution to student outcomes and satisfaction has found that peer learning in an online setting has an even more significant impact, likely due to the reduced interaction with teaching staff that online learners sometimes experience. The less direct communication, involvement, or mediation available from instructors, the more students rely on peers for direction and information. For online learners, lack of interaction can lead to feelings of isolation, insecurity, and doubt along with dissatisfaction with a course, instructor, and overall experience. Student reporting low interactivity in their online learning experiences tend to disengage from content and drop out at higher rates (Yuan and Kim, 2014).

This chapter explores opportunities for librarians to create, facilitate, and encourage peer-to-peer learning for online learners, utilizing a variety of methods taking place in both virtual and physical spaces. It will cover:

- Facilitating P2P interactions and learning communities in online courses and cohorts.

- Creating peer eMentoring programs to promote success and retention for mentor and mentee.

- Models for establishing in-person P2P support for online learners.

## Facilitating Peer Interactions and Creating Online Learning Communities

### Online Participation *Is* Online Learning

According to Hrastinski (2009), online participation *is* online learning. Citing meta-analyses covering 164 studies, 194 independent academic achievement effects, 82 different learning outcome measures, longitudinal studies of 26 online courses, and surveys of over 1,400 online students, Hrastinski determined that participation and peer learning are beneficial and necessary for effective online learning. Online learner participation equals enhanced learning, improved retention, significant positive impact on achievement, higher self-efficacy, and increased satisfaction (Hrastinski, 2009, 79). If we look at Bloom's learning pyramid in Figure 4.1, we see active, participatory learning is where most of the action takes place.

Fostering relationships between online learners keeps them motivated and engaged—it keeps them participating. These relationships should be seeded and grown throughout the session, course or cohort. Essentially, an active learning community must be created. The oft-cited McMillan and Chavis (1986) found that the most important aspects of feeling a sense of community with other learners are (1) a sense of group membership, (2) feeling influential within the group, (3) trust that your needs can be met within the group, and (4) shared emotional connection. Let's look at ways a librarian can support the connections and participation needed to forge online learning communities.

### A Sense of Group Membership

Students interact and participate in their learning in complex and abstract ways. Requiring a number of discussion board posts and responses is a fine way to motivate students to check in with their classmates. Requiring them

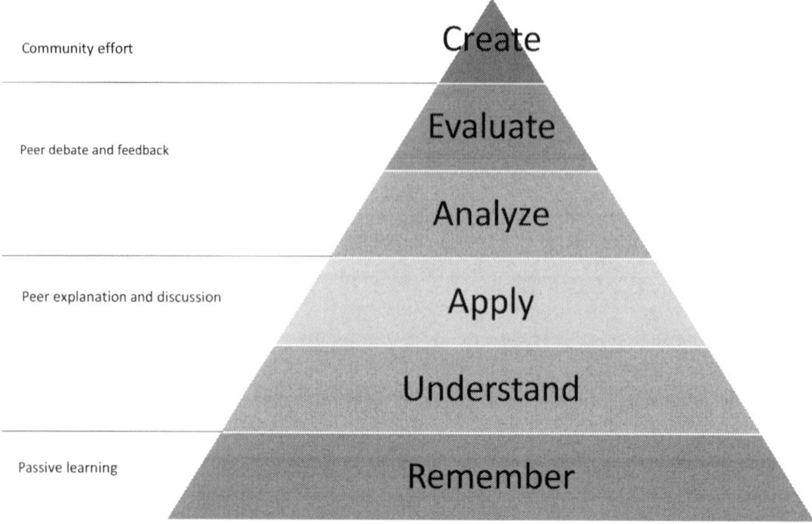


**Figure 4.1**   Bloom's pyramid with peer learning level indicated.

to read others' posts carefully, reflect on them, critically think about the content, and apply peers' ideas and suggestions to their work is even better. Create group membership by:

- Asking learners to find supporting evidence in written, video, or pictorial form for a peer's opinions or observations.
- Creating a video response to a peer's written post.
- Having students create and share polls or surveys to learn about each other and varying opinions and experience.
- Assigning discussions or assignments that encourage personal sharing of past experiences, culture, or values, which foster shared emotional connections.

### Feeling Influential within a Group

Learners feel influential when their opinions and thoughts are heard and acknowledged, when they help others, and when their input is incorporated into course or group projects. To facilitate this feeling, design group activities that assign roles and tasks such as leader, communicator, editor, etc., that allow peers to be influential in a recognized way and that encourage a sense of accomplishment when the group's task is complete. Provide an outline defining the roles and their contributions, or ask the students to create the definitions themselves. When the project is completed, have them self-reflect on how their and others' contributions helped the project be successful.

Also consider a PAL approach to help peers learn directly from each other by matching peers up to edit and review assignments before final submission. Encourage them to provide constructive criticism as well as praise. Provide guidelines for the evaluation to ensure a positive, controlled experience. Peergrade and Flipgrid are popular web-based tools that enable peer review and feedback in virtual environments.

## Trust That Their Needs Can Be Met in the Group

Some of the activities already mentioned, such as group work with specific roles and peer evaluation, should contribute to this need as learners find they are empowered and are improving their learning through peer interaction. Relating P2P work to real-life problems, experiences, or needs will provide an even richer connection. The community will be more powerful if members believe their needs can be met by the group. Creating assignments that result in content or products that can be used practically and outside of the classroom such as guides, white papers, infographics, wikis, websites, tutorials, digital stories, or maps is one way to accomplish this. Another is to clearly explain how the roles, relationships, and interactions inform personal and professional relationships. Through the online learning community, the student is gaining negotiation and debate skills, gathering intercultural communication tools, and building leadership experience. Examples of how new skills and knowledge would be listed on a résumé, CV, or graduate school application will also motivate learners to continue to engage.

Making it easy to interact will also meet the individual needs within the group and help prevent individuals from being marginalized or left behind. Interaction strategies that take advantage of mobile phones are a great example. Adapting discussions and assignments to platforms with good mobile apps or responsive web design so learners can participate anytime, anywhere can help meet student communication needs. Creating spaces where learners can and want to interact is also important. Are the discussion boards active and welcoming? Are disagreements resolved through academic discourse? If online learners look for physical meeting spaces, are you able to provide that? We'll look at in-person learning circles for online learners later in this chapter.

## Emotional Connection

An online learning community requires that people get to know each other, create sustained connections, and collaborate in a way that provides value and empowers the learners. All of this creates emotional connection.

However, participation is not always equivalent to collaboration or cooperation. It's a social dialogue, an attempt to learn and create together, a mutual effort to fashion a meaningful experience. That means there are conflicts, disagreements, and debates. All these complex interactions create bonds. These types of interactions demand further engagement and stretch critical thinking skills. The community is working toward the combined goal of completing the course and mastering the content. The challenges along the way create as many emotional connections as the ultimate triumph. Allow healthy debate, facilitate peer coaching and help seeking, and urge learners to overcome issues together. All of these things build community.

## Creating Learning Communities

As we've seen, fostering participation and P2P interaction are necessary for effective online learning. Creating online learning communities is also a critical component of that work. Let's look further into online learning communities and how online librarians build them.

Evidence shows that online students feel less isolated, have higher rates of retention, and express more satisfaction with their learning experience when they feel connected to others through learning communities (Pigliapoco and Bogliolo, 2008; Rovai, 2001). Rovai (2002) identified the most essential elements of community as: "mutual interdependence among members, sense of belonging, connectedness, spirit, trust, interactivity, common expectations, shared values and goals, and overlapping histories among members" (4). Yuan and Kim's (2014) guidelines for facilitating the development of learning communities in online courses provide excellent insight into the best practice for educators to make and maintain these critical supporting structures. This work can be done over a sixteen-week course or an hour-long synchronous information literacy session.

- Clearly explain the purpose and benefits of the community-building activity and how it will positively impact the students. This could be in a library-run discussion board, at the beginning of an information literacy session, before a tech mentor workshop, or the first week of an online course.

- Focus on building community throughout the session or course from beginning to end.

- Community is built by learners and educators. Providing your own introduction, sharing your goals and struggles, and being honest with answers and advice strengthen community connections. Those canned searches during one-shots aren't exactly honest examples!

- Facilitate connections within the community through personal introduction, shared expectations, and relating course work and discussion topics back to real-life scenarios. Having learners share practical examples of the content or working together to create plausible scenarios addresses the most complex levels of learning.

- Design tasks and assignments that provide opportunities for learners to be community members, facilitators, and leaders. This promotes investment and empathy. Building models, developing examples, and imagining together helps create a sense of accomplishment in community members and shows fellow participants can meet the academic needs of the individual members.

- Flip classes so that reading and watching happens asynchronously while discussion and interaction happens synchronously with the learners altogether in a virtual space, if possible.

- Promote spaces such as online courses, websites, LibGuides, Twitter feeds, and live chats that support virtual interaction both synchronous and asynchronous.

- Acknowledge the contributions of individual learners and share their impact.

There are very practical ways to help build an online learning community in a course you may be embedded in or supporting but not designing the curriculum for directly. It can be as simple as turning your dedicated discussion thread in the LMS into a learning community by facilitating peer help seeking and answering, thereby building a transferable FAQ. Or perhaps creating a Facebook or Reddit group where students share questions, challenges, tips, and tricks for the class and its assignments. The library may be able to embed library student assistants, library school interns, or "library ambassadors" in the online course or cohort that function as information literacy and reference peer mentors or tutors. The library should train these peers and provide them with tools to facilitate interaction and discussion between learners regarding information literacy skills. This might include evaluating sources, avoiding confirmation bias, synthesizing information, and citing evidence. Libraries that offer online peer research services or peer chat reference are also well posed to support online learning communities. Creating peer services for sustainability is discussed more in Chapter 5.

## Developing eMentoring Programs

### A Brief History

Virtual mentoring programs, often referred to as eMentoring in the literature and online, have been around since the advent of email. An excellent definition of eMentoring can be found in Single and Muller (2001, 108). In the following passage, we might replace the term "protégé" with "mentee," but the sentiment remains the same:

> A relationship that is established between a more senior individual (mentor) and a lesser skilled or experienced individual (protégé), primarily using electronic communications, and that is intended to develop and grow the skills, knowledge, confidence, and cultural understanding of the protégé to help him or her succeed, while also assisting in the development of the mentor.

Substantial early eMentoring programs leveraging the new email technology of the time included Hewlett Packard's 1994 Email Mentoring Project, which paired K–12 students with professionals to help with science fair projects and class assignments along with Dartmouth College's 1995 Women in Science E-Mentoring Program (later MentorNet) that paired over 11,000 undergrad and graduate women with female professionals in the STEM fields (Single and Single, 2005). Eventually going beyond email, programmers at MIT created MOOSE Crossing in the late 1990s, a text-based virtual environment in which children eight to thirteen learned coding in a "self-directed, peer-supported environment" (Bierema and Merriam, 2002, 216). Since then, many successful eMentoring programs have been established by K–12 organizations, universities, and nonprofit and for-profit companies. Some of those responsible for these programs have created sophisticated algorithms and computer programs to assess impact and effectiveness as well toolkits and guides on how to implement programs.

eMentoring has the potential to cross barriers of race, gender, geography, age, and hierarchy that are rarely crossed in traditional mentoring relationships. By offering a "safe" context for establishing relationships between diverse parties, eMentoring holds the potential to erode some of the traditional power dynamics that tend to structure mentoring relationships. Sproull and Kiesler (1991) have suggested that markers of social status are less visible in electronic communication, thus rendering them less important to the overall exchange.

A recent systematic review of eMentoring found that it was more cost effective than in-person mentoring, provided additional and more timely support for mentees, and created an opportunity for private and honest discussions on sensitive topics (Chong et al., 2019). Is also enhanced knowledge assimilation, facilitated the formation of social bonds, and enhanced collaborative learning. An exciting aspect of eMentorship is that mentors and mentees that would not normally gravitate to each other based on social, ethnic, gender identification, or other demographic information choose each other more easily because the pairing is not a visual process. Depending on the communication platforms the participants choose or are instructed to use, participants get to self-disclose as they feel comfortable rather than worrying about judgment based on visual factors. Of course, self-disclosure is a major part of creating the bond that makes mentorships work. But in an eMentoring program, it is a personal choice what to disclose, and any immediate bias or anxiety about pairing can be mitigated through the process.

## Benefits of the eMentoring Program for Mentee and Mentor

### *For the Mentee*

eMentees experience similar benefits as those in a traditional, face-to-face mentee relationship:

- Developing communication skills.
- Building lasting relationships.
- Building confidence and identity.
- Improving self-efficacy.
- Increased motivation for learning and achieving.

In addition, researchers have shown that eMentoring programs offer mentees a relationship unhindered by the barriers of social status and less susceptible to the negative impact of hierarchical power structures that limit communication in traditional mentoring programs (Good, Halpin, and Halpin, 2000; Headlam-Wells, Gosland, and Craig, 2006). eMentoring relationships have been shown to have higher rates of open, sustained dialogue over face-to-face mentoring relationships (Smith-Jentsch et al., 2008). All of these factors make eMentoring relationships potentially more impactful and sustainable than in-person programs for underrepresented groups and populations that experience cultural or social bias. Technology skills and experience communicating in a professional and/or academic manner through email or other online platforms will also be enhanced.

### *For the Mentor*

Studies indicate that peer mentors, tutors, and helpers knowingly experience benefits within the P2P relationship. Beltman and Schaeben (2012) found that mentors most frequently report the benefits as:

- Satisfaction with helping other students with problems or difficulties.
- Passing on their own knowledge.
- Developing friendships.

- Developing confidence.
- Gaining leadership skills and experience.
- Getting to know other/new students.
- Learning about their own organization and available resources.

Mentors also report that they would have found being a mentee beneficial and wish they had the same opportunity in their educational career. eMentors experience the same lack of sociocultural barriers as eMentees, potentially providing individuals that would not normally see themselves as mentor types or that may be overlooked in face-to-face programs an opportunity to mentor those like and unlike themselves. Sustaining communication also appears to be easier for eMentors.

## Planning an eMentoring Program

Planning an eMentoring program can be a daunting task, but the library is an ideal place to host such an effort. It can match mentors and mentees across disciplines, school districts, socioeconomic, ethnic, cultural, and demographic lines. It is not tied to a single platform, which allows mentors and mentees to determine their own communication mode or choose one that best suits the program. The library also benefits from creating strong relationships with career centers, peer connection centers, local school districts, businesses, and/or entrepreneurial centers. Table 4.1 provides guidance on planning an eMentoring program from the library. Here are just a few possible eMentoring programs libraries might facilitate:

- Pairing mentors who have completed online degrees or courses with those just starting or having trouble in the same programs or courses.
- Pairing mentors who have finished senior capstone projects, thesis, or dissertations with students embarking or struggling with that process. This can be in the research, writing, or defense phase of the process.
- Pairing K–12 mentees with college student mentors in STEM, arts, or social science fields to discuss preparation, career selection, and college life.
- Pairing first-generation college students with upper classmen mentors to help navigate processes and bureaucracies.
- Pairing newly hired graduate mentors with students working toward the same degree or similar positions for help in preparation and course selection.
- Pairing mentees in online business courses, start-up workshops, or innovation challenges with successful entrepreneurs, developers, and inventors.
- Pairing returning learners of nontraditional age with similar mentors who have completed the process to provide advice and support.

**Table 4.1   Planning an eMentoring Program**

| Setting Goals/Outcomes for the Participants | |
|---|---|
| Subject matter assistance | Mentor: Gain experience teaching, training, and sharing subject matter expertise. Evidence of knowledge and expertise for future employers. |
| | Mentee: Improved mastery of subject matter, ability to discuss and think critically about subject matter. Finds safe place to express concern about learning and mastery. |
| Connection to resources | Mentor: Improved understanding of available resources and how to access them. Able to express available resources to mentee and peers. |
| | Mentee: Connection to writing, tutoring, health, cultural, and social resources is improved. |
| Career development/ professionalism | Mentor: Professional experience in subject matter, training, interpersonal communication, and relationship building. |
| | Mentee: Growth in professional and interpersonal communication skills. Introduced to more senior or knowledgeable peers promoting aspirational goals. Demonstrated commitment to knowledge and skill building. |
| Network development/ advice | Mentor: Learns to make connections between peers, mentors, and mentees. Builds professional and/or academic network. Demonstrated commitment to helping others and social justice. Learns to self-disclose and create new relationships across sociocultural boundaries. |
| | Mentee: Grows academic and professional network. Learns to make professional connections. Learns to self-disclose and create new relationships across sociocultural boundaries. |
| Selecting Appropriate Mentors and Mentees | |
| Time/availability | Mentor and Mentee: Ensure participants have the time to fully participate throughout the length of the program and to attend orientation. If they are a student, will there be time assigned within the class to build this relationship? If they are a TA, intern, faculty, or staff person, will their work schedule ensure they have set aside time to be fully engaged in the mentoring relationship? |

*(continued)*

**Table 4.1** (*continued*)

| | |
|---|---|
| Knowledge/ expertise/ experience | Mentor: Is this person sufficiently knowledgeable, experienced, or have the expertise to answer the mentee's questions, assess the mentee's progress, and provide suggestions, additional resources, or advice based on that assessment? Are they able to identify when other support personnel, educators, or peers need to brought in to meet goals or address unforeseen issues? Are they capable of assimilating the training information and autonomously applying it to different situations with the mentee? |
| | Mentee: Is this person willing to put in the work to gain new skills, communicate regularly, and think critically on relevant subjects? Do they understand the time and effort this relationship will take to be meaningful? Are they capable of learning the communication platform and using it regularly? |
| Motivation | Mentor: Is the mentor intrinsically motivated to help, support, and/or teach others? Are they empathetic? Are the outcomes or benefits clear to them? Are they being incentivized meaningfully, through class credit, financially, or as preparation for a future career? |
| | Mentee: Is the mentee motivated to invest in the relationship? Are the outcomes or benefits clear to them? Do they know how much time to expect from their mentor? Are they able to self-disclose area of struggle and success? Will they be open to the mentee's communication? |
| **Preparing the Participants** | |
| Pairing | Mentor and Mentee: Pairing can be done using a variety of criteria, such as:<br><br>• Subject matter interest and expertise<br>• Professional goals/type of work<br>• Shared interests or preferences<br>• Complimentary characteristics<br>• Mentoring type<br>• Communication style<br>• Availability<br><br>Pairing can also be done through random selection using a database or online randomizer, through selection by mentor or mentee based on a set of disclosed characteristics, or through a program director using personal knowledge to match up mentor/mentee. |

(continued)

**Table 4.1** (*continued*)

| Training | Mentor: The mentor should receive training on the following: |
|---|---|
| | • Recommended communication platform and style<br>• Program expectations<br>• Available resources<br>• Available professional networks<br>• Interpersonal communication<br>• Generational and cultural diversity training<br>• Tips for providing feedback and coaching<br>• Reporting requirements and processes for suspected abuse, harassment, or possible mental health issues<br>• Conflict resolution |
| | Mentee: The mentee should receive training on:<br>• Recommended communication platform and style<br>• Program expectations<br>• Where to go for help if there are issues with the mentor<br>• Guidelines on expected behavior with mentor—respect, courtesy, acceptable language<br>• Tips on how to receive feedback and coaching |
| **Setting Communication Guidelines** | |
| Style and frequency | Mentor: Mentor should be clear what the expected communication style of the program is—polite and informal is suggested. A frequency minimum should be set (weekly or monthly check-ins), and ways to handle too frequent communication or overload should be offered. Mentor should be sure to keep appointments. |
| | Mentee: Mentee should be clear what the expected communication style of the program is and how frequency check-ins or meetings should occur. Program manager should be available to mentees with concerns regarding mentor communication or frequency. |
| Approach | Mentor: Facilitate frank and open discussion and self-disclosure to build relationship. Reach agreement with mentee on next steps and expectation within the relationship. Open and consistent interactions are important for success.<br>Mentee: Be open, honest, and devote meaningful time and effort to learning about the mentor and sharing information about themselves. Mentees should always be polite, but also they should be themselves. |

*(continued)*

**Table 4.1**   (*continued*)

| Platform | See eMentorship Communication Platforms, Pros and Cons, Table 4.2 |
|---|---|
| **Assessing the Program** | |
| Record frequency, length, type, and purpose of interactions | Ask both the mentor and mentee to record frequency, length, type of interaction, and motivation for initiating or not initiating communication. Did they meet via Skype once a week for an hour? Or email occasionally, whenever help was needed? This will allow comparisons between mentoring pairs and with individuals not in an eMentoring relationship. |
| Surveys | Surveying mentors and mentees for factors such as increase in subject matter expertise, confidence, self-efficacy, change in practice, professional growth, personal growth, desire to continue relationship, if they would recommend the program, etc., will help refine the program and assist the mentors in becoming better partners in the process. |

## Communicating in an eMentoring Program

How the mentor and mentee will communicate affects the way their relationship will be built and sustained. The communication platform becomes an important choice that can be made by the program director or the mentor and mentee as part of the pairing criteria or during negotiation of their meeting schedule. More textual platforms or ones that utilize avatars may be beneficial for mentees that are hesitant to self-disclose or come from under-represented populations that may fear bias. Social platforms might work best for programs requiring frequent communication between busy people that prefer mobile phones. eMentoring through email could help develop a professional writing style in mentees not used to communicating in that mode. Let's look at the pros and cons of some popular vehicles for mentor/mentee communication in Table 4.2.

## Facilitating In-Person Interaction for Online Learners

### Learning Circles

In the last few years the concept of learning circles has gained traction in public libraries. This is a wonderful development for online learners, particularly learners with limited technology and English-language skills. Learning

**Table 4.2    eMentorship Communication Platforms: Pros and Cons**

|  | Pros | Cons |
|---|---|---|
| Learning management system (LMS) | Mentees already in the space regularly for course work<br><br>Can be customized to meet need of course or program<br><br>Allows for communication to be potentially regulated by instructor or program manager<br><br>Low bandwidth requirements<br><br>No need to share personal emails or social handles | Requires students to log in to a siloed system<br><br>May not be where they communicate regularly<br><br>Requires institutional support and academic technology assistance |
| Web-conferencing software (Skype, Google Hangouts, etc.) | Allows for face-to-face, audiovisual communication<br><br>No institutional support needed for one-on-one sessions<br><br>Helps promote communication skills in a professional environment<br><br>Real-time sharing and collaboration in documents or other apps as mentoring session is held<br><br>May not need to share personal emails or social handles | Video aspect may be intimidating to some users<br><br>May require some technical expertise that certain users may not have<br><br>May require more bandwidth than some users have access to<br><br>May require users to create and remember unique account |
| Social media platforms (Facebook, etc.) | Many participants may already be using the space regularly for communication | Customization limited<br><br>Social handles likely need to be shared, which may be worrisome early in the relationship. Or new handles will need to be created. |

*(continued)*

**Table 4.2**   (*continued*)

|  | Pros | Cons |
|---|---|---|
|  | May make participants more comfortable if they are familiar and used to communicating on the platform<br><br>Optimal for mobile users<br><br>Requires low bandwidth | Privacy may not be assured or may not be perceived by participants<br><br>May require some technical expertise that certain users may not have |
| Email | Many participants may already be using the space regularly for communication<br><br>Helps promote communication skills in a professional environment<br><br>Easily share documents, images, videos with short time-lapse<br><br>Requires low bandwidth | Less interactive than some other communication platforms<br><br>Younger participants may not use email very regularly<br><br>User needs to share email address, which may be worrisome early in the relationship |
| 3D virtual world | Highly interactive, may promote engagement<br><br>Allows face-to-face interaction without anxiety or fear of judgement as participants can create avatars<br><br>May allow for sharing of digital objects, program, or concepts that other platforms do not allow | May require technical expertise that certain users may not have<br><br>May require more bandwidth than some users have access to<br><br>Some 3D environment may be clunky or hard to navigate, which can distract from the interaction.<br><br>May require users to create and remember unique account |

circles offer a physical space for students in an online course to gather each week, discuss the course content, and help each other study to complete course work.

As an early adopter of this format, the Chicago Public Library (CPL) has run learning circles for patrons since 2015 in partnership with P2PU. The

CPL offers computers, spaces, and a librarian facilitator for each 90-minute learning circle session, with six to eight meetings per course. Courses are generally chosen from freely available MOOCs and have included courses on personal finance, creative writing, Python coding, and American Sign Language. The CPL found that 45 to 55 percent of online students participating in a learning circle complete the MOOCs they sign up for, over three times the number of students who enroll in MOOCs that complete them on their own (Vercelletto, 2017, 18). The CPL attributes the success to the supportive, social environment created in the learning circle. Learning circle participants noted that peer interactions motivated and encouraged them, contributing their success to "knowing that others face similar experiences, not just me," and "having meeting with classmates kept me meeting expectations" (Fellows, 2018, 5). The CPL librarians welcomed a new way to interact with patrons and the ability to create relationships with them throughout the course period.

For those interested in creating learning circles at their institution, there are many guides and best practice available. Highly recommended is P2PU's Learning Circle Facilitator Handbook, which provides timelines, facilitation tips, and templates of activities and marketing materials. Here are some considerations when choosing to engage in learning circle facilitation:

- Determine your organization's ability to dedicate space and technology 90 minutes a week for six to sixteen weeks per course.
- Choose a course that meets the needs of your community, is freely available, and can be completed in the timeframe.
- Some recommended providers for MOOC courses are Codecademy, Coursera, edX, Khan Academy, MIT Open Courseware, Saylor, and Udacity.
- Ensure that technology requirements of the course can be met by your community or institution (are there additional software downloads, accounts to create, etc.?)
- Review course material for quality and relevance.
- Consider what peer discussion and activities will work with the course content.
- Ensure course assessments and outcomes are meaningful and appropriate for the community.
- Identify existing communities and supporting materials on this or similar courses.

This type of facilitation is easily adapted to school and university libraries. Creating a space for students near campus in an online course to meet, help each other, and speak to a librarian would be an excellent undertaking for an embedded librarian or one responsible for supporting large GE courses taught in online or hybrid modalities, especially ones with high drop/fail/

withdraw rates. When physical learning circles are not possible, try creating library-supported online learning circles utilizing web conferencing tools such as Google Hangouts in conjunction with social media.

## Peer Technology Education

Peer technology education is another way libraries are bridging the digital divide. Aside from providing access to computers and the Internet, group classes on technology are the most common digital divide–bridging mechanism. Important for public libraries, most Americans affirm this focus for libraries: 94 percent of Americans believe public libraries should "offer programs to teach people, including kids and senior citizens, how to use digital tools such as computers, smartphones and apps" (Horrigan, 2015). Group classes may be taught by librarians, interns, or peer technology specialists. Peer technology instruction is also an opportunity for high school and college students to gain volunteer experience, community members to give back, and for stay-at-home parents and retirees to socialize and stretch their teaching muscles. Some libraries also use it as a volunteer opportunity for the mentor to work off fines. Peer technology help can also be provided one-on-one by scheduled appointment or through drop-in hours.

When creating and promoting these classes, make sure to address the patrons' needs using their own words rather than the technical terms some may find intimidating. Examples include:

- Create a Job-Winning Résumé! (Microsoft Word class)
- Build a Budget Spreadsheet for Free (Google sheets class)
- Create a Photo Slideshow for Family and Friends (Google Photo, Flickr, or PowerPoint class)
- What's a Hashtag, Again? (Introduction to Twitter)

It is also useful to have two peer instructors in a group technology training session, especially for beginner level sessions. This allows for one person to lead the group, likely providing a demonstration on a computer, while the other is free to walk around and help those having trouble keeping up. Switching half-way through gives instructors and learners more variety and keeps things lively.

In school and academic libraries, peer technical assistance can take the shape of peer workshops on difficult to use software such as SPSS or AutoCad or assistance using required tools such as the LMS. Peer teachers or mentors in these areas may be compensated as student assistants, provided credit as interns, or given priority usage of high-demand library spaces or equipment. Facilitating peer meet-up groups to support the usage and development of virtual or augmented reality equipment, sound and video creation suites, and fabrication technologies such as 3D printing is an excellent use of library resources and has proven successful at many institutions. The best way to get meet-up groups started is to observe who comes in regularly to use these spaces or equipment and then start up a conversation with them. Encourage them to invite others in their classes or peer groups that are interested in the technology. Providing snacks for the meet-ups always helps!

It's possible that your library has resident experts that have earned online degrees, achieved microcredentials or certifications online, or have taken courses on popular platforms such as Udemy, Coursera, or Codecademy. Promote that on librarian profiles or on Ask Us pages to encourage online learners to contact them. In these interactions they would function not only as librarian experts but mentors with similar life experiences and challenges. At minimum, encourage library employees who have online learning experience to disclose that during interactions with online learners, to help learners feel comfortable and understood.

## Conclusion

P2P interaction, learning, and mentoring are critical to the success of online learners. Peer interaction done well prevents feelings of isolation, increases retention, builds confidence, and helps learners see the relevance and applicability of the subject matter. There are many methods libraries may employ to facilitate and support these peer interactions and relationships. This includes developing learning communities online and on-site as well as building virtual eMentoring programs where mentors and mentees can cross sociocultural boundaries to find help and encouragement. To bridge the digital divide many students struggle to overcome, provide peer tech support for software and hardware, marketed in a way that speaks to the learner's need. Hopefully, this chapter has inspired you to apply some of these ideas and also to imagine totally new ways libraries can build and encourage the supportive, challenging, boundary-busting peer relationships and communities or that online students need to fully realize their potential.

## References

Beltman, Susan, and Marcel Schaeben. 2012. "Institution-Wide Peer Mentoring: Benefits for Mentors." *The International Journal of the First Year in Higher Education* 3(2): 33–44.

Bierema, Laura L., and Sharan B. Merriam. 2002. "E-Mentoring: Using Computer Mediated Communication to Enhance the Mentoring Process." *Innovative Higher Education* 26(3): 211–227.

Chong, Jia Yan, Ann Hui Ching, Yaazhini Renganathan, Wei Qiang Lim, Ying Pin Toh, Stephen Mason, and Lalit K. R. Krishna. 2019. "Enhancing Mentoring Experiences through E-Mentoring: A Systematic Scoping Review of E-Mentoring Programs between 2000 and 2017." *Advances in Health Sciences Education* 25: 1–32.

Fellows, Michelle. 2018. *The Learning Circle Experience: Findings from the P2PU Participant Survey.* Seattle: Technology & Social Change Group, University of Washington Information School.

Good, Jennifer M., Glennelle Halpin, and Gerald Halpin. 2000. "A Promising Prospect for Minority Retention: Students Becoming Peer Mentors." *Journal of Negro Education* 69(4): 375–383.

Headlam-Wells, Jenny, Julian Gosland, and Jane Craig. 2006. "Beyond the Organisation: The Design and Management of E-Mentoring Systems." *International Journal of Information Management* 26(5): 372–385.

Horrigan, John B. 2015. *Libraries at the Crossroads.* Washington, DC: Pew Research Center. www.pewinternet.org/2015/09/15/libraries-at-the-crossroads.

Hrastinski, Stefan. 2009. "A Theory of Online Learning as Online Participation." *Computers & Education* 52(1): 78–82.

McMillan, David W., and David M. Chavis. 1986. "Sense of Community: A Definition and Theory." *Journal of Community Psychology* 14(1): 6–23.

O'Kelly, Mary, Julie Garrison, Brian Merry, and Jennifer Torreano. 2015. "Building a Peer-Learning Service for Students in an Academic Library." *portal: Libraries and the Academy* 15(1): 163–182.

Pigliapoco, Erika, and Alessandro Bogliolo. 2008. "The Effects of Psychological Sense of Community in Online and Face-to-Face Academic Courses." *International Journal of Emerging Technologies in Learning (iJET)* 3(4): 60–69.

Rovai, A. P. 2001. "Building Classroom Community at a Distance: A Case Study." *Educational Technology Research and Development* 49(4): 33–48.

Rovai, A. P. 2002. "Development of an Instrument to Measure Classroom Community." *The Internet and Higher Education* 5(3): 197–211.

Single, Peg Boyle, and Carol B. Muller. 2001. "When Email and Mentoring Unite: The Implementation of a Nationwide Electronic Mentoring Program." In *Implementing Successful Coaching and Mentoring Programs*, ed. L. Stromei, 107–122. Cambridge, MA: American Society for Training and Development.

Single, Peg Boyle, and Richard M. Single. 2005. "E-Mentoring for Social Equity: Review of Research to Inform Program Development." *Mentoring & Tutoring: Partnership in Learning* 13(2): 301–320.

Smith-Jentsch, Kimberly A., Shannon A. Scielzo, Charyl S. Yarbrough, and Patrick J. Rosopa. 2008. "A Comparison of Face-to-Face and Electronic Peer-Mentoring: Interactions with Mentor Gender." *Journal of Vocational Behavior* 72(2): 193–206.

Sproull, Lee, and Sara Kiesler. 1991. "Computers, Networks and Work." *Scientific American* 265(3): 116–127.

Vercelletto, Niko. 2017. "CPL, Learning Circles Help Learners." *Library Journal* 142(11): 16–20.

Wojcicki, Susan. 2020. "YouTube at 15: My Personal Journey and the Road Ahead." YouTube, Official Blog. https://youtube.googleblog.com/2020/02/youtube -at-15-my-personal-journey.html.

Yuan, J., and C. Kim. 2014. "Guidelines for Facilitating the Development of Learning Communities in Online Courses." *Journal of Computer Assisted Learning* 30(3): 220–232.

# CHAPTER FIVE

# Help Them Connect with You: Deploying Effective Online Communication Tools

## Introduction

Online learning can be an isolating experience. Without a physical tie to instructors, fellow students, or a campus, learners feel adrift. We've established that interaction and engagement with teachers, content experts and peers, and inclusion in an online learning community lead to retention and success in online learning. However, even with the use of interactive LMS elements and required discussion boards, it is difficult to establish connection in virtual learning spaces. Online learners must navigate complex library websites without the possibility of just popping into the library to ask a question. They may rely totally on virtual services despite varied degrees of technological know-how. If information literacy instruction modules and librarian-supervised discussion boards are available in the online course, they may not be required or utilized. Taking communication to the virtual spaces online learners inhabit regularly and willingly can build community, enhance learning, and increase engagement.

This chapter presents some of the latest thoughts on providing help to students coming to the library's web portal for answers to reference questions. It also explores successful communication strategies and projects using social media platforms for information literacy instructors and librarians involved in the learning process. I've always been a fan of Zipf's (1949) principle of least effort when designing online services, assignments, and communication strategies. That is, online users, like all patrons, will most likely seek the path of least effort and greatest convenience, avoiding "unnecessary" work whenever possible (Poole, 1985; Rubin, 2004). When figuring out how best to communicate with online learners, it may help to think of it in these terms: keep it simple, make it fast, take it to them.

## Keep It Simple: Building Websites for Online Learners

"Using a library Web site to access resources should not be more trouble than it is worth; otherwise, users will have no qualms about turning to the open Web."

—Dominguez, Hammill, and Brillat, 2015, 100

It's difficult to imagine how a short section of one chapter can portray communicating to users through the library website when entire books, entire series even, are dedicated to the creation of websites, and improving usability. I would never presume to collapse the immensity of that knowledge into a few pages. Instead, let's focus here on what usability measures are most important to online learners and ways to include online-only learners in assessing those features.

### UX Studies and Redesigns

Libraries seem always to be in a state of website redesign. Surveys, card sorting, focus groups. It's wonderful that we're a profession so dedicated to making users happy. How can we assure our online-only users are included in these studies?

Surveys promoted on your website homepage, by social media, in LMS or MOOC classes, or mass-emailed are more likely to reach online students. Links may be sent directly to online instructors with a request to share and be disseminated in virtual reference and instruction sections. In addition to surveys using Survey Monkey, Qualtrics, or LibWizard, free virtual card-sorting programs like OptimalSort (www.optimalworkshop.com), uzCardSort (uzilla.mozdev.org/cardsort.html), or xSort (Mac only, xsortapp.com) can help capture the navigation organization desired by online students. Reach out to online degree programs at the university to recruit students for virtual focus groups held through the organization's web conference applications such as Zoom, Team, Hangouts, or Skype. You may also consider adding slide-outs on your webpages and eResources sites recruiting online-only learners. Make sure when creating user stories or personas that an online-only learner persona is included. Talk to one (or many) online users before assuming to know what behaviors they exhibit, pain points they experience, or tasks they need to complete.

## Content

It's rare to find a library website that values brevity—that is, doesn't have an essay on every possible variation, exemption, side note, and vague possibility regarding most resources, services, and spaces. Note: If a student has to read three paragraphs to know how to use ILL, they will likely find another article to use or pirate it on Google. Simplification is golden. So, do we really need a suite of webpages or an entire LibGuide just on distance library services? If there's a link labeled "Distance Students," how do I know it applies to me or my course? Will an online student necessarily identify as a distance student, especially an international student? The whole thing feels a little . . . disenfranchising.

When at all possible, collapse websites about distance student services where they belong—interspersed with other sections on how to get a book the library doesn't have, how to access eResources off-campus or generic Ask Us pages. If there are distinctly online programs, address the program by name in a guide or site, as students may be more comfortable associating themselves with their major or program rather than as "distance students." If you're attempting to assist students in a MOOC, use the name of course or platform to steer students to the right place.

## Analytics

My favorite web analytics tools are Google Analytics (click paths, time on page, OS/device info), Google Event Tracking (track downloads, video plays, and embedded elements), CrazyEgg (confetti maps showing how different segments of users interact with areas of your page, scroll maps), and Heat-Map (metrics of where people hover and click on your site). Together, these build an incredibly powerful picture illustrating how people use the library's site, navigate it, how long they scan content, if they scroll, what their click path is, and what page they leave the site from. Are users visiting the site from remote locations getting to what they need quickly? Are they misdirected or hitting the back button often? Do they explore promotional images or links? What type of OS or device are they using? CrazyEgg confetti maps (www.crazyegg.com, monthly subscription required) segment users by factors such as operating system, device type, referring website, new or return visitor, and show you exactly what those type of visitors clicked on. Analytics can quickly show how many truly "distant" visitors the website hosts in a given period and what pages they use most often.

## Responsive Design

A best practice to adopt for all website users, who in ever-growing number access websites from their phone whether they take online classes or not, is to build a responsive website. W3Schools.com has an excellent introductory module about responsive design. Take the time to make your site device-agnostic. Constantly test it yourself—you don't need the different devices to do so. To see how pages display on various mobile devices, use the Chrome browser's Developer Tool, choose a device type, and navigate to various pages on the site, as seen in Figure 5.1. You may be surprised how unusable the website is on an iPhone SE or Pixel.

## Accessibility

Some online-only students are learning online due to issues in mobility or disabilities that make it difficult to visit campus or learn in a traditional classroom. This makes them even more vulnerable to marginalization and being left out of usability personas and testing groups. Check with your campus or city accessibility center to find volunteers of diverse capabilities for focus group and usability studies. Don't just test that your sites are screen

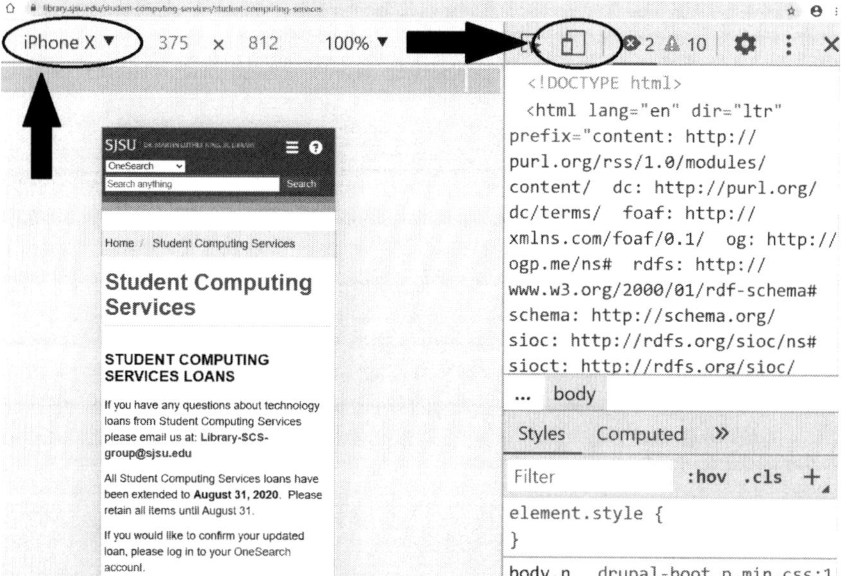



**Figure 5.1** Use the Chrome browser's Developer Tool to toggle between desktop and mobile versions on a website. Choose different device types to assure compatibility across mobile types and dimensions.

readable; make sure their structure conforms to accessibility best practices by creating good headings and navigation structure, shortening navigation lists, and writing comprehensive alternative text for images and GIFs that is read within the correct structure of the site. Maintain good contrast between text and background. And offer well-structured, accessible PDFs as an alternative to multimedia content. Follow W3C standards, found at www.w3.org /WAI, in all that you do with your website to keep it accessible for everyone.

## Make It Fast: Providing Virtual Chat Reference

If Zipf is correct, people will generally seek the most convenient way to meet their information needs. Once a website search has been tried and found lacking, patrons turn to the Ask Us options. For online users, that's a phone number, email, or chat link. Chat has found a home in libraries as the most viable replacement for real-time interaction with a library expert and generally preferred by patrons over other types of virtual reference services. Studies show that students choose chat over all other forms of virtual reference, mostly based on convenience (Connaway, Dickey, and Radford, 2011).

In response, libraries have tried a wide variety of chat services over the last decade or two. In-house, peak-hour chat, and 24-hour consortia chat. Clickable links, slide-outs, and pop-up widgets. Chat staffed by librarians, staff, students, or even robots. We've tried it all! And rightly so. Analysis of reference statistics from these decades of chat found that from 1977 to 2012, questions via chat have become more complex and more likely to be reference-based questions than those received at the library's physical reference desk (Maloney and Kemp, 2015). Yet some institutions have found chat service to be so underutilized and difficult to staff that they consider reducing hours or ending the service altogether. So how can libraries realize an acceptable return on investment with chat? Recent research has made it pretty clear—a little prompting is needed.

### Proactive Chat Widgets

Proactive chat boxes prompt users to ask questions by sliding or popping within a webpage, giving a visual indicator and friendly message reminding users help is available. Originally developed for online businesses, these boxes have been adopted in other industries, including higher education and libraries. In 2013, Rutgers University Libraries made the decision to position a new proactive chat box "at the center of the users' research space," that is, in a central location on all their webpages (Maloney and Kemp, 2015, 960). Before adding proactive chat to their site, approximately seven chat questions came in a day. The first day the box became available they received forty-three inquiries through chat. In the next two years researchers found that chat questions not only exceeded on-site questions by number, but were also of greater quality and complexity by a significant margin.

Zhang and Mayer (2014) at John Carroll University Library found that after implementing a proactive widget that prompted patrons to ask a question after searching their website for 3 minutes, chat reference went from comprising 3 percent of all reference questions to 21 percent. Of the more than 1,000 questions asked during their six-month study, 70 percent of all questions were initiated by the widget prompt and of those, 74 percent were reference or research related and 25 percent directional. In comparison, patron-initiated questions were 57 percent reference and 41 percent directional. The University of Tennessee found that while embedding a proactive chat widget on their eResources page did not increase their traffic by as much as other libraries, the quality and importance of the questions was so high compared to their static widget that a review of their web content management system was warranted to assure better integration of the proactive widget on the library's homepage (Fan, Fought, and Gahn, 2017). It's increasingly obvious that the future of reference is in online, proactive chat.

There are many proactive chat widget options out there, most geared toward serving online businesses. A free one that integrates easily into web platforms such as WordPress and Drupal, allows customization, and saves transcripts is PureChat. Another option used by libraries is ZenDesk, formerly known as zopim, which has a free Lite version available. For an additional ~$150/year you can add multiple operators, customize your widget, and add set triggers (prompts based on defined actions like time spent on a site and return visits). Libraries will also find a proactive chat widget option available through their LibChat subscription with SpringShare. It would be prudent to work out the kinks of your virtual chat service through a free version or free trial before investing in any particular product.

Whatever you choose, consider the following when implementing your proactive chat widget:

- Choose the right pages: proactive widgets work best on homepages, A–Z database pages, and database search pages. You may also want to embed them on LibGuide homepages or other site depending on your analytics.

- Wait for it: you want to be helpful, not overbearing. Give them to time to read and click on their own first by setting the trigger to somewhere between 10 seconds and 3 minutes. You may want to do some user testing of your own or review your Google Analytics data to determine the right amount of time before triggering.

- Don't make them wait too long: if a response via chat isn't available in 3 minutes, the user should be informed and an email follow-up sent. If at all possible, communicate wait times with the user, and ask if they would like you to contact them when you're available.

Once you're virtually chatting with a patron, there are behaviors known to increase the user's satisfaction with the transaction (Baumgart, Carrillo, and Schmidli, 2016; Radford 2006). Remember, for a user who does not or cannot come to the library, this is their main source of interaction with you.

- Listening: patrons report high satisfaction rates when they interact with someone who asks clarifying questions, listens carefully to their requests, and asks follow-up questions.
- Providing instruction: there is a persistent correlation between user satisfaction and the amount of instructions a user gets on how to perform the search or operation suggested.
- Building rapport: when operators provide encouraging comments, use humor or informal language, and share information about themselves, they build a trust and rapport with the user that increases patron self-disclosure and satisfaction with the interaction.
- Mirroring user behavior: When the user adds emoticons, abbreviations, and shortcuts into your chat conversation, you should too. This mirroring of behavior will reduce anxiety in the user and promote open communication, potentially deepening the reference interview and the instructional opportunities of the interactions. This also helps build rapport with the user.
- Greeting and closing: patrons that are greeted at the beginning of the chat, asked if they need anything else, and welcomed to use the chat function again have higher satisfaction rates.

## Staffing a Proactive Chat Service

After embedding a proactive chat widget across your most popular pages, you'll likely find a need to expand your chat staffing well beyond regular librarian and staff hours. Recently, I've had discussions with colleagues in the California State University system who reported removing proactive widgets from database search pages because their library could not handle the number of chat questions coming from these boxes. Libraries have often used students at information or reference desks to supplement staffing needs, and much analysis has been done regarding these transactions. Less is available on peer effectiveness in virtual chat reference.

At California Polytechnic State University San Luis Obispo, a review of student worker chat reference transcripts found the "LibRats" (their endearing name for student reference and instruction workers) were "knowledgeable and congenial" in their interactions (Bodemer, 2014, 171). Lux and Rich's (2016) analysis of transcripts and user ratings at Bowling Green State University found: "Student assistants successfully assisted chat users in 88% of their transactions, and they received more expressions of appreciation from chat users than librarians received" (31–32). However, librarians did outperform student workers on correctness and completeness of answers and building rapport with users. One of the greatest challenges for student assistants was known item searches—a level of reference question many would consider perfect for students to take on. It seems that giving up too soon when not finding the known item was a bigger issue than not providing instruction during the sessions, a conclusion that would go against many existing expectations. And a good place to start training for student workers.

The best way to improve peer (and employee) virtual reference transactions is increased training in the behaviors needed for successful interactions online. Standardizing reference provider training to include the competencies described by American Library Association's Reference and User Services Association *Guidelines for Behavioral Performance of Reference and Information Service Providers* should help (ALA, 2008). Best practices suggest training operators for these behaviors according to the standards as outlined in Table 5.1.

**Table 5.1   Training Goals Mapped to Reference and Information Service Provider Guidelines as Published by the ALA's Reference and User Services Association (2008)**

| RUSA Standard | Service/Training Goal |
| --- | --- |
| 1.0 Visibility/ Approachability | • Set proactive widget to prompt >10 seconds on website<br>• Have operator readily available during "online" times |
| 2.0 Interest | • Greet patron in a timely manner<br>• Check in with patrons and use encouraging remarks as they move through the search and discovery process |
| 3.0 Listening/ Inquiring | • Identify patrons' information goal or objective<br>• Ask clarifying questions<br>• Restate objective to assure understanding |
| 4.0 Search | • Work with patron to determine best search strategy and resource<br>• Instruct patron on how to perform the search while assisting<br>• Use most relevant database or resource rather than favoring a single tool based on comfort |
| 5.0 Follow Up | • Ask patron if the objective has been achieved or question answered<br>• Inquire about additional assistance<br>• Invite patron to use chat services again |

For online librarians, increasing the availability and reach of virtual reference services is critical to serving our online populations. Expanding the staffing models to add peers not only increases available hours for chat, but also virtual working opportunities. Does the student assistant need to be in the library to provide virtual chat assistance? Using virtual chat reference to employ online-only students or provide credit to virtual interns further expands your online impact and the enfranchisement of online students.

## Chatbots

All of this may lead some of the more technology-minded of us to ask: do we really need staffing at all? Can't we just use bots to answer these questions? Chatbots have been hailed as customer services' newest golden child by many in private industry. Their potential for machine learning and real-time interaction with no staff cost make them a corporate mecca. Chatbots' place in libraries have become less clear in recent years. In the 2000s and early 2010s many libraries in the United States and abroad were piloting chatbot projects. *Library Technology Reports* dedicated an entire issue in 2013 to the idea titled "Streamlining Information Services Using Chatbots." Yet, only a few of these chatbot pioneers persist today, and none of them have taken on chat services as originally predicted. It's worth it to take a few minutes to explore what's still out there, why it hasn't caught on, and what might be still to come.

### UCI ANTswers

ANTswers (escholarship.org/uc/uci_libs_antswers) is UC Irvine's experimental Interactive FAQ, released in 2014. ANTswers runs on a remote library server and is accessed through a page on their library's website. The chatbot was implemented with chatbot software Program-O, editing software Notepad++, and minimal experience with HTML, CSS, Javascript, and AIML. Users need to use fairly specific language with ANTswers for success, but it can provide short answers to inquiries about library services and show you to the correct library URL. However, many of the library's pages require authentication before you can view content, a major barrier to access.

### UNL Pixel

Pixel (pixel.unl.edu) is an experimental chatbot being tested at University of Nebraska–Lincoln Libraries. Developed using AIML (Artificial Intelligence Markup Language) and launched in 2011, Pixel can answer questions about library services and resources. This bot can handle more natural language questions than ANTswers and will walk you through several questions to get the right answer. Pixel serves up answers with the corresponding webpage from the library.

### . . . Or Make Your Own!

Using Google's free chatbot development application Dialogflow and an iframe on a Drupal page, two virtual interns recently built a chatbot demo for San Jose State University Library named KingBot. Currently, the answers are still simplistic, but we can see the beginning of a useful help tool built with minimal coding knowledge. For a small fee, use Kommunicate to integrate Dialogflow into a LibChat widget and provide enhanced content such as images and live links. See the demo at library.sjsu.edu/chatbottest.

Although sophisticated chatbots can be built to ask clarifying questions or learn how to, it's difficult to imagine them offering on-the-fly instruction on the use of complex search terms in library databases. A significant investment in programming and teaching the chatbot would need to be made—potentially worth it, although upkeep could be overwhelming. Chatbots can certainly learn to mirror the behavior of users, but they're ability to build rapport is less clear. Considering the hesitancy librarians express regarding trained peers providing reference assistance, I'm not sure bots will be taking over virtual reference anytime soon. But don't take my word for it—build your own and see! The libguide at libguides.sjsu.edu/librarychatbot explores a variety of best practices and resources for building a chatbot for your library.

## Take It to Them: Engaging Online Users with Social Media

We've already discussed the need for online learners to engage with others and feel part of a community in order to succeed in their educational endeavors. It promotes deeper learning, increases retention, and helps students feel they are taking away something concrete from the class or experience. Since the inception of social media platforms, educators have experimented with methods that create interactivity, develop critical thinking, and spur great discussions. Social media has the potential to take online learning beyond even the in-class equivalent by bringing engagement, community, and discussion to students where they already live and communicate.

Twitter, Instagram, Facebook, Snapchat, YouTube, TikTok, Twitch, WhatsApp, Tumblr, HouseParty, YouNow, Reddit, Pinterest . . . and by the time this book is published there will be three more social media platforms people flock to for communication, information, and entertainment. Not all platforms are appropriate for academic interactions due to their design, their data policies, or the communication styles platform users adopt. But boxing up social media as nonacademic, distracting, time-wasting, or unscholarly does a terrible disservice to those you are trying to reach online. Social media is valuable for many reasons:

- Real-time communication
- Designed for peer-to-peer (P2P) interaction
- Media-centric
- Succinct
- Readily available on mobile devices
- Part of the users' regular habits
- Peer ratings/votes/likes
- Available for a larger community
- Available over time, after class ends
- Easy for quick interactions like retweets, reposts, comments
- Creates sense of community

In this section we'll examine current opinions on the ways social media can and should intersect with learning. We will also look at some successful social media integrations used by online librarians and what lessons we can draw from these experiments that can be applied across platforms—even ones that don't exist yet.

## Platform Popularity

It may surprise you that recent Pew surveys have found more Americans across all age demographics have used YouTube above all other social media platforms (Pew Research Center, 2018, 4). Its popularity may be attributed to the variety of content, prevalence in Google search results, or the ability to use it without an account. Regardless, nearly three quarters of all Americans have used YouTube and 94 percent of those between eighteen and twenty-four years old use the site. (So, consider posting all of your video tutorials there, ASAP.)

Although Facebook is second to YouTube in overall usage, it has far more daily users (Pew Research Center, 2018, 5). Nearly 80 percent of all Americans eighteen to fifty use Facebook, and of those 74 percent report using it at least once a day. Facebook reports 2.27 billion monthly users globally as of the third quarter of 2018 (Abbruzzese, 2018). It may feel like every college kid you know is on Snapchat or Instagram these days and it's true—the same survey found 78 percent of eighteen- to twenty-four-year-olds report actively using Snapchat and 71 percent use Instagram. Twitter rounds out the big five with 45 percent of eighteen- to twenty-four-year-olds using the site. How many times a day do you think people are visiting your LMS or library website?

## Facebook

Researchers at Pennsylvania State University and Pacific Northwest National Laboratory found that students preferred using Facebook to communicate over discussion forums in Coursera MOOCs. "Facebook was an attractive place for them to stay actively and longer" (Zheng et al., 2016, 420). MOOC students reported feeling a better sense of a collaborative community, felt the instructor was more present on Facebook, and found it more convenient. Instructors of these MOOCs perceived the use of Facebook in the class as improving student retention, creating community, fostering creativity, and a great place to promote their class. This held true for courses in art, software-based geographic mapping, and creativity and innovation. It is likely that the same outcomes would arise in large online courses at any university, as the difficulty of creating community and getting timely responses on an LMS discussion board could be similar. Public library language and technology courses should also take advantage of the community-building communications dynamic of Facebook.

Owen and Nussbaum's 2017 study comparing student post quality and engagement with Facebook in two University of Nevada introductory psychology courses also found positive results in using Facebook for discussions. The instructors created a private Facebook group and invited the class participants to join. Students appreciated the "usability, accessibility and convenience associated with Facebook," citing the ease of posting on a smartphone, ability to get instant notifications, and lack of clicks to get to the right place to post when assignments were due (260). The authors also analyzed the Facebook postings, which showed a high degree of analytical argument construction compared to students posting on other social media sites. Even more insightfully, students discovered the social media site could create a community of practice that included their class peers, stating: "Being able to connect with my peers on [a] social networking site made me realize that there is a multitude of ways to connect not only on a personal level, but also on an educational level," and "It was interesting to me that this seemingly trivial social network site could be used in a more serious way" (261).

## Twitter

There are multiple ways to interact on Twitter. Users can post tweets, like tweets, re-tweet other's posts, reply (comment) on a tweet, and mention or @ another Twitter user to call attention to a tweet they might be interested in. Twitter's current 280-character limit forces users to be precise with their thoughts and comments, while also encouraging the posting of images, videos, and GIFs to get the point across. It's easy to search for user-created hashtags, and a hashtag can be quickly created for a class, discussion topic, or class project by a librarian, instructor, or discussion group. Hashtags such as #SJSUEDU100 #GroupMaslow, indicating course and group name, can be used to create more context for the post. Twitter maintains a number of useful APIs that even beginner developers can use to curate, follow, or embed content into LMS pages, WordPress blogs, or other web portals.

Looking again at Owen and Nussbaum's (2017) Twitter research, they found that students assigned to small group discussions appreciated the ease of posting even if they sometimes found following the discussion initially confusing. As one student put it: "Twitter made it easier and faster for me to participate in discussions just because I could send out my tweets while I was out. I liked that it only took me a few moments to put my two cents in" (259). Students imagined other ways to use the platform, such as identifying tweets that exemplified the different parenting styles presented in a class lesson, then retweeting them to the class with a topic hashtag for credit. A librarian could use the course hashtag for an online Q&A thread or to blast out research tips. Instructors and students might monitor the tag from anywhere with their mobile device, adding their own questions, thoughts, and tips to the mix.

On-site and online students have found Twitter discussions increase interaction in a class, increase perceived learning, and build online course community (Thoms and Eryilmaz, 2015). Since tweets can have multiple hashtags, students may address multiple community groups and topics with each post, making commenting for class a potentially community-engaging activity. This encourages them to make connections between academic concepts and the real world. Twitter has been shown to improve student motivation and engagement, increase interactivity, and lower barriers to student "publication" and risk taking in their self-expression (Carroll and Dasler, 2015, 490). The low character limit and informality of tweeting make students more comfortable in joining in discussion and engaging personally with the community.

## YouTube

Libraries will be familiar with YouTube for hosting instructional content or video blogging. Many videos celebrating Banned-Book Day, illustrating Boolean search techniques, and promoting summer reading programs have been posted by libraries around the world. Instructors may host lectures, create playlists of topical videos, or use excerpts from YouTube to highlight art, culture, or politics. These are all excellent ways to use YouTube for communication.

Reportedly the most used social media platform, we might imagine many studies would be available that analyze the use of YouTube in the online and physical classroom and the platform's use for learning generally. Although it does appear in peer learning studies (as we have seen from Chapter 4) and is often mentioned when analyzing flipped-classroom models, YouTube doesn't get the research attention it deserves based on its usage. Very recently, sociological and business studies on how YouTubers entice consumers or use instructional methods to teach things like makeup application or skin care have emerged. These studies explore YouTube as a communication vehicle, product engagement tool, and a place to analyze sociocultural interaction both in the video and in the comment section. YouTube is a fascinating anthropological artifact! But evidence of the platform's ability to create more formal learning communities or course-specific communication outside of expert content delivery is not readily apparent.

However, it is likely the students you're working with anywhere on earth, at any age, will be familiar with this platform. This familiarity can be harnessed by encouraging users to become peer experts and share their knowledge through video making; to create playlists that visually describe and explore concepts; and to interact with videos from others in the class, including your own. Perhaps an assignment asking a student to "pitch" various aspects of information literacy or share their progress in a language or on a coding assignment would be a good place to start with the platform. Easily shareable, YouTube content can also be embedded in or posted to most all other media platforms. And anyone with a smartphone can participate in this powerful knowledge transfer.

## Pinterest

Pinterest often gets dismissed as a website dedicated to party planning and home remodeling, a derision likely stemming from a majority female user population—not the preferred demographic in the male-dominated Silicon Valley. However, Pinterest is uniquely qualified as a platform to share visuals in a curated library, while also exposing the user to similar content. All without the hassle of copious fake news and grating ads. Not only can libraries use Pinterest to share unique content such as digital archival collections with links back to the source, librarians and instructors can develop assignments with it to help students gain visual and social media literacy skills through media curation, description, and citation. Users do this by creating "pin boards" where they pin or repin images, videos, and other media based on their own themes, using a dedicated text area to describe or comment on the pin. Other users interact by following, repinning, and commenting on pins.

Decker (2016) found that when students were assigned a topic, trained to use the site, and provided some technical assistance with "pinning," they were able to achieve visual literacy skills as described by ACRL's *Visual Literacy Competency Standards for Higher Education*. They did this through selecting and evaluating images that placed historical figures in context (in this case artists from the Harlem Renaissance), including images of original works, buildings and streets, events, clothing, and contemporary media. By asking students to create a "digital representation of the life of their person-age," on a virtual pin board, the instructor and librarian led the students through a visual journey re-creating the context of these artists' lives, which could be shared with classmates and the entire world through this online platform (Decker, 2016, 79).

## Reddit

Reddit claims itself to be "the front page of the internet." Per Reddit's own Google snippet: "Reddit gives you the best of the internet in one place. Get a constantly updating feed of breaking news, fun stories, pics, memes, and videos just for you." However, its demographics skews young males, and Reddit frequently finds its hands full policing inappropriate and controversial subreddits (user-made group message boards). Think GamerGate. Despite some people's perceptions of Reddit, there are certain features to Reddit that make it a very interesting platform for communicating with users, especially online learners looking for quality answers and content from you and other members of a class or community. Users can make public or private subreddit boards with a name of their choice such as r/uscgeo102, a subreddit for USC's GEO 102 course. Each subreddit is hosted by a moderator (you or assigned students) and governed by a posted list of rules regarding board etiquette. You can moderate as much or as little as you like.

Although there are few if any studies regarding the use of Reddit in an online class, I have spoken with librarians who have successfully piloted it in large online courses. The idea is generally to create a subreddit where a librarian-to-student and/or student-to-student FAQ is evolved using actual student questions and answers. Questions are posts that anyone in the class can answer, which are then up-voted or down-voted depending on their quality or relevancy, allowing the best questions to rise to the top of the list. Responses to each post are also voted on, allowing the best, most informative answer to rise to the top of the responses for each question. It's also possible as a moderator to make a "sticky" post at the top of a subreddit or to make your reply to any post "distinguished and sticky" to keep it at the top.

Creating this kind of peer up-voted FAQ is a particularly good strategy if you're planning to support a large number of sections of the same online class. The opportunity for P2P learning is immense, and the FAQ will be available beyond the course end date, to be reused and refined by future students. You can ask students to request access to the private board or make it open for all with just a link to the subreddit.

## Citation Management Tools

For online librarians looking for ways to provide feedback on student sources, citations, and bibliographies or to support collaborative citation evaluation, Zotero and Mendeley are great free options. Although not technically social media platforms, they offer collaborative capabilities for students and educators that make them important and useful communication tools.

*Mendeley.* Mendeley is a robust free citation management tool that is downloaded locally to a computer, installed as a browser add-on for quick citing, and added as a plug-in to your word editing software. It is easy to make groups in Mendeley, which allows sharing of a citation set and peer commenting. A recent two-year research trial at the College of William and Mary School of Education utilizing Mendeley as a collaborative learning tool for small groups found it an easy-to-use virtual meeting space (Khwaja and Eddy, 2015). The trial assignment in the study asked students to collectively annotate and critique a research article. The students then collected additional relevant literature, synthesized the works, and wrote a group policy brief. The initial task of highlighting and annotating a research article is of great interest to librarians assessing information literacy achievement. Mendeley keeps track of which user adds which annotations so the instructor can also provide individual grades in this group assignment. The authors described Mendeley as "a powerful platform for researchers as well as students . . ." (Khwaja and Eddy, 2015, 20). Since the trial was done over consecutive years, they were able to use feedback from year one to iterate the assignment and training in year two. Based on student input, the most important factors for success included:

- Smaller groups so that everyone had enough content to comment on during the annotation phase. Otherwise latecomers were unable to complete assignments—a typical issue with discussion boards and group collaborations.

- An online training module on using the software needed to be available throughout the term as a refresher to students.

- Providing clear learning goals regarding using the software so students could connect their training to practical outcomes.

- Making a space for peer mentorship from those with more knowledge of the software to help newer users.

*Zotero.* Zotero works similarly to Mendeley, in that it requires a local download to a computer, browser plug-in and/or word editor add-on. It also offers the ability to make collaborative groups on the platform. Students are able to share research resources or create group bibliographies, which can be particularly useful in large online courses that rely on group research projects. Librarians and instructors can access bibliographies to leave comments regarding sources. Kuglitsch (2015) described using Zotero for group research in a course as particularly rewarding for librarians and a way to provide students concrete take-aways: "the librarian can situate communication about research resources within a tool of actual long-term research utility to students. Students benefit more from leaving college with the skills to use an open-source information management tool rather than honing skills useful only within an institutionally bound CMS" (70).

## So Many Platforms . . .

Table 5.2 offers examples of class projects, assessments, discussions, and assignments that can be done over various social media platforms. Most require that the user create an account, which may take additional instruction. Students may want to create a new/additional username for the platform if they don't want to link their academic life to their social media persona or reputation. You will want to provide an alternative to students who have objections to a particular platform or possibly lack access from their country.

## Conclusion

When communicating with online patrons, it is important to remember that information seekers look for the path of least effort. Keep websites simple, accessible, and device agnostic. Don't make users struggle to find information relevant for them by siloing it onto "distance student" webpages or burying it in walls of text. Use tools like Google Analytics and CrazyEgg to find out what content different user types look for and click on. Include online-only learners in UX studies so your website design reflects their needs, too.

We know that a majority of users choose virtual chat reference based on convenience and that users may prefer asking complex reference questions via a chat box rather than the physical reference desk. Employ proactive chat widgets to prompt user inquiries, and train those answering the inquiries according to established guidelines and known best practices. Libraries can provide virtual interns an opportunity to work or get library experience by answering virtual chat reference questions—research shows that students answer chat inquiries nearly as well as professional staff. Libraries should analyze transcripts to assess and improve services.

When communicating with online learners, it is imperative to create interactive, engaging experiences and to build online learning communities

**Table 5.2　Suggested Methods for Incorporating Social Media Platforms into Online Learning and Engagement**

| Platform | Example Uses |
| --- | --- |
| Facebook | • Create a classroom community on Facebook where users interact and ask you questions. You can post reminders and tips on the page.<br>• Poll your students through Facebook to quickly ascertain how they're feeling about the class, assignments, topics, etc.<br>• Ask students to find and share with the class "fake news" or "bots" on Facebook to help teach information and digital literacy. Have them discuss why they believe it is fake and what the content or bot is trying to achieve.<br>• Support students in finding a "community of practice" on Facebook that addresses a topic or career they're interested in. What did they learn from the community? |
| Twitter | • Assign a class hashtag and ask students to tweet/retweet relevant thoughts and tips about the class there. Encourage students to submit questions and answer others' inquiries. They can use screenshots and images to illustrate issues and solutions.<br>• Have student search for relevant tweets on their topic and retweet under their own hashtag. They can rate the quality of the user and tweet for credibility.<br>• Students can follow politicians in their region to analyze their posts and updates for information on local agendas, issues, and debates.<br>• Have students identify and follow professionals in their field of study. What are the latest issues in their field, and what are people saying about them? |
| YouTube | • Students can create a tutorial showing their research or writing process to share with the class via private URL or post publicly on the site. Comments should be turned on for private videos or off for public ones, if there are privacy concerns.<br>• Ask students to build a playlist of existing videos that address a concept or idea, such as APA citation or writing a literature review. Have them share with the class via URL or embedded video.<br>• Create a class FAQ by having students find and post videos that helped them finish their assignment or research paper. Make the playlist public and reuse in future courses. Allow students to continue to add to and curate the FAQ over time. |

(continued)

**Table 5.2** (*continued*)

| Platform | Example Uses |
|---|---|
| Reddit | • Create a Reddit board that is shared with members of the class across multiple sections and semesters. Ask students to post their own questions and answer peers' questions. The best questions and answers will be upvoted on the board by peers, librarians, or instructors. Remember to assign a moderator.<br>• Create a Reddit board as a discussion board for the class. Each post can be a question from the instructor. Answers are replies that can be upvoted by others in the class. |
| Tumblr | • Tumblr is especially useful for mental health, social justice, gender studies, and pop culture analysis/curation. Students studying in these areas may want to create a Tumblr focused on a particular issue or concept. They can post text, images, video, or GIFs to their feed at regular intervals as an alternative to discussion board posts. Others in the class can repost their content with additional text or materials to build on the concept. Create class- or topic-specific hashtags for quick discovery. |
| Pinterest | • Have students create "pin boards" that explore a person, place, or event. Ask them to "pin" images from archives, other pin boards, or online sources that help their peers visualize and learn about the topic. Although text is limited, ask students to note and/or link to the original source so others can further explore the topic.<br>• Assign the creation of a Pinterest bibliography. Users pin articles, blogs, images, videos, and other media types that influenced or contributed to a research, engineering, design, or art project. Student should provide as much information on the provenance of the pin as possible. |
| Instagram | • To explore copyright issues, ask students to identify images on Instagram that may be violating copyright or that are licensed under Creative Commons. Have them share under a class hashtag. Ask them to discuss how they determined the copyright violation and why it matters. Others can repost and comment to discuss.<br>• In groups or individually, students choose a historical or literary figure to create an Instagram feed for. What would that person see and do in their daily life? What would have inspired them? Use class hashtags to follow the project as well as tags relevant to the figure to contribute to any community of interest that exists on the platform. |

*(continued)*

**Table 5.2**   (*continued*)

| Platform | Example Uses |
| --- | --- |
|  | • Students can capture images that show the progress of a project or steps of science experiment in order to share with the instructor or class. Ask students to compare results of art or design projects with each other and the "insta" community. |
| Twitch | • Have students identify Twitch videos that are particularly helpful for learning a game. Students should describe the methods the Twitch host uses that make the video successful as a learning tool. How can they apply that to their own visual and video creations?<br>• Groups of students designing games, software, or working on any project online can record themselves on Twitch, capturing the group process of communication and troubleshooting. The instructor can grade the group interaction and individual contributions to the process. |
| LinkedIn | • Assign students to build a profile that highlights their experience, academic achievement, and coursework related to their future career goal. Students should add peers to their network and endorse each other's skills as appropriate.<br>• Ask students to identify three individuals on LinkedIn that they want to have an informational interview with about their future career. What made the individual's profile compelling? How can they incorporate that into their own career plan and LinkedIn profile? |
| ResearchGate | • To better understand the research lifecycle, students can look up a research article they found especially useful this term on ResearchGate and analyze the following: What are the metrics like for this paper? How has the academic community responded to this work? Does it have many citations/views? What does that indicate about the source?<br>• Assign graduate students to identify a researcher/author in their field of study. Using ResearchGate ask them to answer questions like: What kind of topics is the author working on? What journals do they publish in? How has their research changed over time, and why do you think that is? |

(*continued*)

**Table 5.2** (*continued*)

| Platform | Example Uses |
|---|---|
| Zotero/ Mendeley | • Use Mendeley, Zotero, or other citation management tools to review student citations and resources before a major research assignment is due. Provide feedback on the platform or separately, depending on the features available. Use the review to suggest better journals, databases, or resources for the research topic.<br>• Assign students to use the citation manager to work on a collaborative literature review.<br>• Ask the group or individual to find a public citation list that is similar to their topic. What articles/works could be included in their review? Why or why not? |

whenever possible. Take help, discussion, content, interaction, and community building to the learners by employing the right social media platform. Grow communities of practice on Facebook, encourage concise discourse on Twitter, and ask students to create helpful videos or playlists on YouTube that can be embedded in an LMS discussion post or anywhere. Librarians and students can collaboratively interact with research papers and bibliographies in applications like Zotero and Mendeley, creating better literature reviews and a lasting resource for students. The rapidly rising TikTok platform and its short-form mobile video format remind us that we will need to engage with new platforms as they emerge and be flexible regarding our communication and lesson plans. Online students using social media platforms feel more engaged in the class, experience a better sense of community, and may be forging critical analytical ties between course lessons, class discussions, and the real world that promotes learning, especially in non-traditionally-aged students.

## References

Abbruzzese, Jason. 2018, October 30. "Facebook Hits 2.27 Billion Monthly Active Users as Earnings Stabilize." *NBC News.* https://www.nbcnews.com/tech/tech-news/facebook-hits-2-27-billion-monthly-active-users-earnings-stabilize-n926391.

American Library Association (ALA). 2008. *Guidelines for Behavioral Performance of Reference and Information Service Providers.* http://www.ala.org/rusa/resources/guidelines/guidelinesbehavioral.

Baumgart, Steven, Erin Carrillo, and Laura Schmidli. 2016. "Iterative Chat Transcript Analysis: Making Meaning from Existing Data." *Evidence Based Library and Information Practice* 11(2): 39–55.

Bodemer, Brett. 2014. "They CAN and They SHOULD: Undergraduates Providing Peer Reference and Instruction." *College & Research Libraries* 75(2): 162–178.

Carroll, Alexander J., and Robin Dasler. 2015. "'Scholarship Is a Conversation': Discourse, Attribution, and Twitter's Role in Information Literacy Instruction." *The Journal of Creative Library Practice*. http://creativelibrarypractice.org/2015/03/11/scholarship-is-a-conversation.

Connaway, Lynn Sillipigni, Timothy J. Dickey, and Marie L. Radford. 2011. "'If It Is Too Inconvenient I'm Not Going After It': Convenience as a Critical Factor in Information-Seeking Behaviors." *Library & Information Science Research* 33(3): 179–190.

Decker, Emy Nelson. 2016. "Pin This: Working with Faculty to Enrich the Classroom Environment via Pinterst." In *E-Learning and the Academic Library: Essays on Innovative Initiatives*, eds. Scott Rice and Margaret N. Gregor, 79–88. Jefferson, NC: Gregor McFarland & Company.

Dominguez, Gricel, Sarah J. Hammill, and Ava Iuliano Brillat. 2015. "Toward a Usable Academic Library Web Site: A Case Study of Tried and Tested Usability Practices." *Journal of Web Librarianship* 9(2–3): 99–120.

Fan, Suhua Caroline, Rick L. Fought, and Paul C. Gahn. 2017. "Adding a Feature: Can a Pop-Up Chat Box Enhance Virtual Reference Services?" *Medical Reference Services Quarterly* 36(3): 220–228.

Khwaja, Tehmina, and Pamela L. Eddy. 2015. "Using Mendeley to Support Collaborative Learning in the Classroom." *Journal of Educational Technology* 12(2): 19–28.

Kuglitsch, Rebecca Zuege. 2015. "Repurposing Zotero for Sustainable Assessment and Scalable Modified Embedding." *Reference Services Review* 43(1): 68–80.

Lux, Vera J., and Linda Rich. 2016. "Can Student Assistants Effectively Provide Chat Reference Services? Student Transcripts vs. Librarian Transcripts." *Internet Reference Services Quarterly* 21(3/4): 115–139.

Maloney, Krisellen, and Jan H. Kemp. 2015. "Changes in Reference Question Complexity Following the Implementation of a Proactive Chat System: Implications for Practice." *College & Research Libraries* 76(7): 959–974.

Owens, Marissa C., and E. Michael Nussbaum. 2017. "Twitter vs. Facebook: Using Social Media to Promote Collaborative Argumentation in an Online Classroom." *Journal of Interactive Learning Research* 28(3): 249–267.

Pew Research Center. 2018. "Social Media User in 2018." http://www.pewinternet.org/2018/03/01/social-media-use-in-2018.

Poole, Herbert. 1985. *Theories of the Middle Range*. Norwood, NJ: Ablex.

Price, Elizabeth. 2018. "Should We Yak Back? Information Seeking among Yik Yak Users on a University Campus." *College & Research Libraries* 79(2): 200–221.

Radford, Marie L. 2006. "Encountering Virtual Users: A Qualitative Investigation of Interpersonal Communication in Chat Reference." *Journal of the American Society for Information Science & Technology* 57(8): 1046–1059.

Rubin, Richard. 2004. *Foundations of Library and Information Science.* New York: Neal-Schuman.

Thoms, Brian, and Evren Eryilmaz. 2015. "Introducing a Twitter Discussion Board to Support Learning in Online and Blended Learning Environments." *Education and Information Technologies* 20(2): 265–283.

Zhang, Jie, and Nevin Mayer. 2014. "Proactive Chat Reference: Getting in the Users' Space." *College & Research Libraries News* 75(4): 202–205.

Zheng, Saijing, Kyungsik Han, Mary Beth Rosson, and John M. Carroll. 2016. "The Role of Social Media in MOOCs: How to Use Social Media to Enhance Student Retention." In *Proceedings of the Third (2016) ACM Conference on Learning@ Scale,* 419–428. New York: Association for Computing Machinery.

Zipf, George K. 1949. *Human Behavior and the Principle of Least Effort: An Introduction to Human Ecology.* Boston: Addison-Wesley Press.

# PART 3

# Building Engagement

# CHAPTER SIX

# Help Them Help Themselves: Information and Digital Literacy for the Online Learner

## Introduction

Librarianship as a profession is dedicated to empowering people with information and knowledge through literacy. That literacy may take on many forms, including reading and writing, teaching and learning, researching and publishing. Librarians teach individuals to inquire, search, evaluate, curate, analyze, create, collaborate, credit, and disseminate knowledge. We help people find connections in a vast global network of information and media.

Whether you're working to address the ACRL's *Framework for Information Literacy in Higher Education*, providing digital literacy to adult populations, following the AASL *Standards Framework for Learners*, or curating tutorials for professionals searching a local corporate library database, you're teaching literacy. This instruction is happening increasingly online, not just in higher education, but in all patron populations as they seek out information and learning in virtual environments and with the expanding suite of web- and app-based library resources. We must make every effort to design instruction for the online user as thoughtfully and intentionally as we do for our on-site students and patrons.

Because all types of libraries and librarians engage in literacy education, this chapter exploring online library, digital, and information literacy instruction purposefully avoids alignment to any particular literacies' framework or standards. Rather, it builds on the theories about information seekers and learners that we've established in previous chapters as especially applicable to those learning online. It does so in the hopes of encouraging all library professionals to imagine how they would apply the strategies, examples, and tools described here to their own practice and instructional design for online learner populations. Let's start by reviewing the concepts we've established so far.

1. Based on the principle of least effort, we can predict that people will seek information through the most convenient, least painful path (Poole, 1985; Zipf, 1949), making that path the one that leads through your library's instructional content must be part of our service and instructional strategy.
2. Active learning, as part of constructivist learning theory, is an established pedagogical approach indicating that students require active, authentic engagement in the learning process to build deep understanding and knowledge (Detlor et al., 2012).
3. Addressing the online learner's need to build community and create connections will improve the learning experience and keep students engaged throughout the process (Pigliapoco and Bogliolo, 2008; Rovai, 2001).

To better apply these theories to online library instruction, this chapter will introduce also the concept of learner characteristics. Presenting instruction to learners in a way that does not connect with them personally, does not fulfill any of their perceived needs, and does not feel authentic will lead to disinterest, dissatisfaction, and a lack of retention (Manwaring et al., 2017). It simply wastes both your time and theirs. Evidence shows that text-based learning in an online environment may be perceived by many students as tedious and disengaged, while interactive experiences based on real-world issues enhance their perceived experience (Boling et al., 2012).

When creating instructional materials, maximize the fruit of your efforts by making sure it is in a format learners are drawn to and presented in a manner that keeps their attention and addresses their immediate and long-term need. Taking the characteristics and preferences of your likely audience into account during instructional design, or in user experience speak, developing content for a likely user persona, sets you and the learner up for success. Researchers have found that design definitely influences engagement (Manwaring et al., 2017; Robinson, Kilgore, and Warren, 2017).

So, creating engaging, relevant, opportunely placed instruction is the goal. There are simply too many competing resources that learners will turn to if yours don't work for them. Let's explore some ways of designing and delivering online library and information literacy instruction that takes into account relevant existing theories and learner preferences while also working to relieve burdens on librarians and improve the sustainability of your instructional programming to online learners. To do so, this chapter will explore:

- Understanding learner characteristics.
- Identifying instructional opportunities.
- Applying approaches that address online learners' needs and preferences.
- Reaching out to partners, collaborators, gatekeepers, and innovators.

## Understanding Learner Characteristics

For decades, researchers have been interested in better understanding the characteristics that define each generation and comparing them to each other. The study of generations, their characteristics, and the effect they have on history is known as generational theory, conceived of initially by Howe and Strauss in their 1992 work *Generations*. More recently, educators have been applying generational characteristics, as they emerge, to teaching and learning design. This is done with the understanding that instruction designed to meet the likely characteristics, preferences, or personas of student populations would be more successful at meeting the learners' needs and expectations (Lim and Kim, 2003; Swan 2004). The practice of considering the characteristics and personas of potential user groups has been adopted in many areas of design, including software, architecture, and user interface/experience design.

As of 2020, the generations school and academic librarians are most likely to encounter in instructional spaces will be Millennials (1983–2000) or Generation Zers (2000–2018). However, the rise in returning students is well documented. Between 2001 and 2015 the number of returning students enrolled in postsecondary institutions aged twenty-five to thirty-four rose 35 percent, and for students over thirty-five the increase was 13 percent (Hussar and Bailey, 2018, 25). And these percentages are projected to increase over the next decade. Additionally, business and public librarians need to create instructional content for adult learners from a variety of generations. Is it possible to reconcile the varying characteristics of generations we serve? And what would they look like applied to the established learning theories already discussed?

Recent studies on Gen Z have found this group to be optimistic, caring about social change, less creative due to declining art education, and that they prefer not to sit through lectures about things they believe can be found on the Internet (Mohr and Mohr, 2017; Seemiller and Grace, 2017). Compare that to the Millennial generation who are defined more by their service/volunteerism orientation, closeness to family and parents, desire to achieve, and willingness to work for that achievement (Howe and Strauss, 2000; Taylor,

2006; Wilson and Gerber, 2008). In both populations, instant gratification, constant digital connection, and an expectation to use technology tools for learning and work are prevalent. Both generations report that they are also interested in making a difference, seeing the results of their labor, being recognized for their contributions, and prefer multitasking.

Although some of these characteristics are unique to generations that came of age after the Internet was readily available via mobile devices, many are similar to the characteristics ascribed to adult learners by researchers such as Knowles (1973, 1984); Westmeyer (1988); and Merriam, Caffarella, and Baumgartner (2007). These adult learner characteristics include a preference for self-directed learning, a desire to apply existing knowledge to learning, wanting new skills and information to be relevant to their own goals, and finding self-reflection important. Looking at these characteristics in Figure 6.1, clearly there are overlapping themes. It's interesting to consider that these populations potentially have many overlapping characteristics that are simply expressed differently by themselves and their observers.

Although the category of "online learner" is too broad to create any meaningful list of characteristics, there is a significant body of research focused on the characteristics of successful online students. These are generally college, middle school or high school students, adults in online training or certification courses, or adults in MOOCs. Figure 6.2 highlights some of the most proven characteristics of successful online learners, according to researchers (Kauffman, 2015; Swan, 2004). These include independence, enthusiasm, high self-efficacy (confidence in ability to perform tasks), internal and/or visual learner, developed communication skill, and technology competence. It also includes high emotional intelligence, such as the ability to control

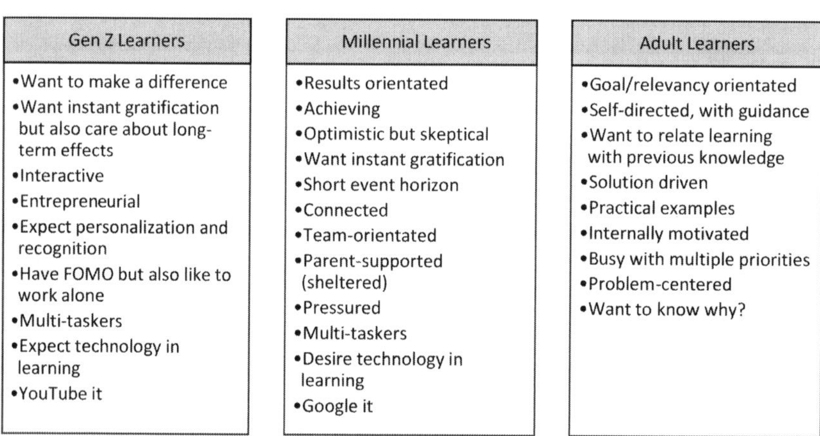



**Figure 6.1**  Learning characteristics: Gen Z learners, Millennial learners, and adult learners.

ones' own emotions and a developed capacity to feel and express empathy for others. Of course, the goal in reviewing these characteristics is not to design toward them, but to understand that these are the skills we want to encourage and develop in online learners. Designing instruction that reaches, engages, and positively impacts those online learners that don't already exhibit these skills or characteristics is part of our challenge.

| Successful Online Learners |
| --- |
| • Independence and capacity for self-direction |
| • Enthusiastic or motivated |
| • High self-efficacy or confidence |
| • Internal/visual thinkers |
| • Good communication skills |
| • Good technology skills |
| • High emotional intelligence |

**Figure 6.2** Characteristics of successful online learners.

Looking across these categories and considering them in conjunction with the three learning principles stated at the beginning of this chapter—the principle of least effort, the benefits of active learning, and the importance of building community and connection on learning outcomes—we may derive some common instructional design approaches to engaging and positively impacting the learner populations we are likely interacting with during online instruction:

- Lessons, activities, and assessments should be relatively short or phased for the multitaskers and busy learners.

- Information and learning objectives need to address a purpose or goal that is relevant to the learner.

- Learning will be more effective if grounded in the learners' own experience or personal interests.

- Learners prefer technology-enriched content, activities, and assessments that are interactive or collaborative, with possible individual pathways to completion.

Of course, these characteristics do not represent all learners in any of these groups; learners, like all humans, are individuals and will have some combination of these and other characteristics. Many studies on generational characteristics largely rely on American or Western populations, so difference according to cultural, ethnic, socioeconomic, and other factors are not highlighted. Whenever you're designing instructional content, making sure it's adapted for non-English speakers, learners with accessibility accommodation needs, and people with differing learning requirements is highly recommended.

The Universal Design for Learning (UDL), developed at the Center for Applied Special Technologies (CAST), is an excellent framework for understanding how these adaptations can be facilitated. The UDL provides guidelines for designing multiple means of representation, expression, and engagement, enabling educators to create an inclusive learning environment and experience. More on UDL design mapped to information literacy outcomes can be found in Webb and Hoover (2015); UDL and creating accessible learning materials can be found at CAST.org.

## Identifying Learning Opportunities

Before we dive into applying the approaches defined above, let's take a moment to consider the importance of identifying learning opportunities. Later in this chapter we'll discuss finding collaborators and partners in instruction, which is certainly a large part of identifying opportunities. However, learning opportunities are anywhere users interact with your organization, services, resources, or people. Every Google search, discovery search, website, tutorial, LMS interface or course shell, webinar, material request, workshop, orientation session, on-site or online information literacy one-shot, chat interaction, email, or phone call is a learning opportunity. And that opportunity may be the only one you'll get to reach the online learner.

Libraries often relegate library instruction to specific webpages or guides, believing that learners will get there through link navigation, librarian direction, or their own searches. This just really isn't the case. If help isn't where learners need it, they will turn to quicker, more convenient sources even if they are seen as less knowledgeable or comprehensive (Oh and Colón-Aguirre, 2019, 883–884). Libraries should strive to insert instruction when and where it is needed. Frequently, libraries make FAQ links or chat widgets only available from Ask a Librarian or Get Help with Your Research pages. This adds an additional burden to the user; not only must they get help, now they need to find where help is, potentially separated from where the question or pain point occurred.

Designing for the online learner means identifying instructional opportunities at the point of need and delivering the right instructional content and format at that point. This may be a traditional course-specific LibGuide or an information literacy instruction module in the LMS that includes video tutorials, discussion threads, and exercises. It might also be an embedded video or GIF on an accounts page or in an interlibrary loan form, a PDF help file on using eBooks with a screen reader in an eBook FAQ, a self-assessment quiz for plagiarism on a citation guide, or a proactive chat widget embedded in a discovery or OPAC record display. Placing the instruction where it is needed and in the most relevant and convenient format is good instructional design.

## Put Library Instruction Where It's Relevant

When considering where to locate instructional content, think real-time relevancy. Tutorials embedded or linked from database pages, discovery systems, and service or resource pages should be targeted to address the immediate need; linking to a long list of tutorials is suboptimal, as is linking to a generic "distance services" page where the user must find the relevant information again. Tutorials on specific databases or tools might also include a note regarding open access alternatives for those without off-site access privileges.

Use terminology familiar to the learner when titling, describing, and adding metadata to tutorials, guides, and webpages. This may mean adopting the vernacular of a particular discipline, instructor, grade level, profession, or vendor (if describing a resource). Very few people know or care what Boolean means.

Consider tagging more generic guides and tutorials with course names or numbers, or resource names to optimize searching while preventing the proliferation of course guides or webpages. A guide on off-site electronic resource access might be tagged with common database and resource names (Academic Search Complete, OverDrive, Westlaw) or vendor names that many learners mistake for database names (Gale, ProQuest, EBSCO). A typical user's search for help might be constructed as: "no results in EBSCO." If your "better searching" video has no metadata about EBSCO and is not embedded in the EBSCO search page, that user might never be connected to it.

## Embedding LTI Tools

LTI (Learning Tools Interoperability) tools are third-party external plug-ins for the LMS that comply with the open standards maintained by the IMS Global Learning Consortium. Users benefit significantly from these tools as they embed content directly in the LMS, eliminating the need for students to leave the native LMS interface or authenticate separately to access resources.

Magnuson (2014) describes three LTI integrations with library content that promote library instruction and student access to resources: (1) EBSCO Curriculum Builder, which allows users to search in the EBSCO Discovery Service for EBSCO content within the LMS; (2) Ex Libris' Leganto Reading Lists tool that delivers electronic course reserves inside the LMS; and (3) SpringShare's LibGuides tool, which uses metadata from LMS courses and LibGuides to match up subject and course guides with LMS course shells, delivering relevant library guides to the student with one click. Additional integrations from SpringShare include LibChat services, LibAnswers FAQs, and LibCal scheduling for office hours.

The steps for these integrations are well documented in the literature; libraries can find support for LTI tool integrations from their instructional designers or LMS administrators. Other LTI examples include Wikipedia, WorldCat Discovery API Search and Retrieval, Gale Virtual Reference Library, and Alexander Street Press, among many others. Harvard's LTI Workshop, available on GitHub at github.com/Harvard-ATG/workshop-lti -basic, is highly recommended for learning more about building, customizing, and integrating LTI tools in your LMS.

## Online Portals

Adding your instructional content to places learners get to through Google searches is another exciting and underutilized opportunity. Taking advantage of Quora, Yahoo Answers, wikiHow, Reddit, and YouTube, which flood the top of search results pages when users enter question-type inquiries into the Google search box, is an untapped dimension of library services. Posting well-designed instruction to these platforms could potentially move your quality library content to the top of any users' search page. Of course, you'll have to get users to rate/like/recommend your content before it will float to the top. Good design can do that for you, too!

## Applying Approaches Designed for Online Learners

> "The most important principle for designing lively eLearning is to see eLearning design not as information design but as designing an experience."
>
> —Cathy Moore

The following approaches are an excellent starting point for planning meaningful interactive, collaborative, technology-enhanced learning experiences during online library and information literacy instruction. These examples and practices attempt to follow current learning theories and address learner characteristics. They are also intended to build the type of skills online students need to be successful—self-efficacy, internal and visual thinking, and communication skills, among others. Hopefully, they are also adaptable, sustainable, and fun!

### Lessons and Activities Should Be Relatively Short or Phased for the Multitaskers and Busy Learners

One way to approach this idea is in the creation of Digital Learning Objects (DLOs). DLOs are discrete content packages that address a single learning objective, activity, or assessment. Some other terms for this might be a learning asset or an Open Educational Resource (OER), although not all DLOs are openly licensed. They are ideally shareable, accessible, interoperable with many platforms, and sustainable. Since DLOs are focused on a single objective or activity, it helps us to keep our format brief and to be intentional about the way users interact with it, what their outcome will be, and where the DLO can best be placed in the learning pathway. Maintaining accessibility and interoperability also ensures DLOs can be placed in multiple learning pathways and so encountered by the largest number of users at the right time in the journey.

### Creating and Deploying DLOs

Aligning DLOs to information literacy standards or learning outcomes and then grouping them into modules inside the LMS is an excellent way to create sustainable and sharable online information literacy content. DLOs can be kept by the library in an LMS course shell shared with all librarians, all instructors, or the entire campus or district. They should be organized by established learning objective or standard, based on the type of population you serve. Alternatively, they can be placed in an open access repository for public access and reuse outside the organization—make sure to CC license them if you do this. Either way, the DLOs are then available to be placed in any online, hybrid, or flipped course, arranged or customized as determined by the librarian and instructor, and reused each time the course is taught.

Start with a set of basic DLOs around introductory topics like call numbers, searching the catalog, off-site resource access, constructing search inquiries, building a thesis statement, performing source evaluation, and basic citation styles. This will serve as a default starter kit for online library and information literacy instruction. A small work group or task force would be responsible for the creation and maintenance of these DLOs. More customized DLOs on topics such as specialized databases, evidence-based practice, and writing a literature or systematic review would be built by librarians as needed and added to the shared set of DLOs. DLOs will likely include video tutorials, html pages, PDFs, mind mapping or brainstorming tools, embedded communication tools, interactive assignments, discussion prompts, quizzes, polls, or synchronous lesson plans. Even if not used for scored assessment, providing quizzes that allow students to self-assess their understanding of the materials are a great tool for instant feedback. ACRL's *Framework for Information Literacy in Higher Education* and AASL's *21st Century Learner Standards* can help guide these efforts. An example of learning outcomes derived from the Association of American Colleges and Universities and ACRL's information literacy guidelines and relevant mapped DLOs are shown in Table 6.1, based on Mune et al., 2015.

**Table 6.1    Example of Information Literacy Learning Outcomes and Mapped Digital Learning Objects (DLOs)**

| Learning Outcome | Mapped Modules and DLOs |
| --- | --- |
| Developing a thesis and topic | Writing a thesis statement<br>• 2-minute video of thesis-writing strategies<br>• Accessible PDF<br>• Three-question self-assessment quiz<br>Finding and developing a topic<br>• Link to online mind-mapping tool<br>• 1-minute video demonstrating tool<br>• Accessible PDF |
| Searching effectively | Choose your search terms<br>• Webpage with search GIFs<br>• Link to online thesaurus<br>Search better faster<br>• 3-minute video of search strategies<br>• Accessible PDF<br>Find peer-reviewed articles<br>• 3-minute video of searching discovery system and databases<br>• Accessible PDF<br>Find newspaper articles<br>• 3-minute video of searching news database<br>• Accessible PDF |
| Evaluating sources | Know your sources<br>• Webpage with table showing scholarly vs. newspaper vs. popular vs. trade sources<br>• Know your source trivia game |
| Applying information to your assignment | Writing an annotated bibliography<br>• 3-minute tip video<br>• Accessible PDF<br>• Five-question self-assessment quiz<br>Writing a literature review<br>• 3-minute tip video<br>• Accessible PDF<br>• Five-question self-assessment quiz<br>Writing a whitepaper<br>• Accessible PDF<br>• Five-question self-assessment quiz |

(continued)

**Table 6.1**  (*continued*)

| Learning Outcome | Mapped Modules and DLOs |
|---|---|
| Writing citations and avoiding plagiarism | Citing in APA<br>• Link to LibGuide with GIFs<br>• Link to eResource or eBook<br>• Eight-question self-assessment quiz<br>Citing in MLA<br>• Link to LibGuide with GIFs<br>• Link to eResource or eBook<br>• Eight-question self-assessment quiz<br>Citing in CMS<br>• Link to LibGuide with GIFs<br>• Link to eResource or eBook<br>• Ten-question self-assessment quiz<br>How to avoid plagiarism<br>• Avoiding plagiarism trivia game<br>• Accessible PDF |

### *Videos*

One of the most common DLOs librarians make are videos. I have to admit, I've spent many years as a librarian on a "make videos shorter" soap box, and I have no intention of stopping now! Tutorial videos should be 3 minutes, maximum. There's a reason that social media video platforms serve short, quick clips that repeat. Because that's what people pay attention to. Many will not need sound, using either titles or intuitive images to indicate what must be done. To address nonvisual learners, create substantive alt-text or provide an accessible PDF help file as an alternative. Recent work by Rush and Stott (2014) focuses on the creation of 1-minute videos to impart core library instruction in digestible bites. This idea is partially constructed on previous work done by researchers like Bowles-Terry, Hensley, and Hinchcliffe (2010), indicating that for Millennials, even 3-minute videos could be considered too long and that the length of the video directly related to viewing decisions. Series such as Message in a Minute (Oviatt Library), the Library Minute (Arizona State University), and One Minute Tips (Old Dominion University) have received positive feedback for the brevity of their delivery.

Some quick tips on making videos that users will click on and finish:

• Videos should be no more than 3 minutes long; digestible bites of information are best.

- Leave off introductions—they are often scrubbed through (fast forwarded by pulling the time indicator forward) or spur users to click on another video to get to the actual content they're looking for.
- Most videos should not require sound to be understood as some viewers will not have access to sound in shared study or community spaces. Closed captioning, descriptive alt-text, transcripts, and/or an accessible PDF help file alternative is a must.

Some great tools for making short video or even animating them to mix things up are:

- Animaker for creating 2-minute animated messages with drag and drop editing.
- Screencast-o-matic for quick screencasts including zoom-ins for emphasis.
- Powtoon to create quick animated lesson using free templates.

### GIFs

Consider a series of still images or GIFs as a possible alternative to video tutorials. Mestre (2012) found that for most library instruction, students prefer images over videos, especially for simple tasks and concepts (266). GIFs are a perfect format for a DLO and can be easily embedded in a webpage or pop-up widget. These short, looping videos have no sound, use simple callouts, and are a format very familiar to younger users. No clicking into a video is required. A series of GIFs that can be scrolled through by the user make more complex actions available for instruction in this format. EZGIF makes free GIFs and provides instructions for new GIF makers. GIPHY's GIFMaker is a popular application for GIF making on a desktop. They can also be made in Photoshop. Make sure to provide substantive alt-text in the html anywhere you use GIFs.

Making short videos and GIFs are also excellent activities to assign students you're working with online or when flipping the information literacy classroom. Learners can show off the information literacy skills they're learning while increasing digital literacy. A GIF or short video might show a search strategy, illustrate how to generate a citation, use callouts to evaluate different resources, or storyboard the development of a thesis topic. You may want to ask learners for permission to share their work with future students as examples—a great opportunity to teach the class about Creative Commons licenses. These DLOs are easily shared through social media or in an LMS. GIPHY and GIPHY Cam are both great mobile applications for making GIFs that most students will have access to via their smartphones.

### Ease of Translation and Transferability

Short, to-the-point videos or GIFs offer the added benefit of easy translation. It's highly likely that your instructional content will reach users with limited English-language skills. This is true in any organization, for any kind of library. If you can portray a concept without language, do it. This is most often possible when teaching tools and processes. For larger, more complex concepts, keep the script simple, and always provide closed captions or a transcript for easy translation. Designing tutorials can be a real balancing act between keeping it graphic to address language and engagement issues and ensuring there is a textual option to address visual impairments. Keep in mind the need to address varying adaptive learning needs and styles. Creating both short visual content and a textual, well-formatted PDF utilizing Web Content Accessibility Guidelines (WCAG) 2.1 as an alternative is the most universal and accessible route.

Depending on your potential audience, designing instruction with the nonaffiliated user in mind might also be appropriate. This type of content seeks to inform learners not associated with your organization, possibly in continuing education or open university program, on literacy concepts, alternative resources, and local options. Again, decoupling organizational processes from instruction will be important. Highlighting open access options, recommending ways to get connected with local libraries, and illustrating methods of circumventing obstacles like paywalls should be addressed. Colocate this type of information with career and professional development opportunities, alumni access pages, or guides for disciplines that offer MOOCs and microcredentials.

## Information and Activities Should Address a Purpose or Goal That Is Relevant to the Learner

This principle should be followed by everyone when creating instructional content, online or otherwise. The learner must feel connected to the goal or purpose and see its relevancy in relation to their own goals or needs. That doesn't require excessive personalization, but rather the librarian should attempt to make a direct connection to learners' assignments, academic career, future profession, or personal growth goal when setting the lesson up.

### Relate to Real-World Needs and Skills

Relate library and literacy lessons to real-world goals and skills. Applied Digital Skills from Google (https://applieddigitalskills.withgoogle.com/s/en/home) provides an excellent example of this. Designed with teachers and librarians in mind, Applied Digital Skills lessons use DLOs to create online learning pathways building real-world skills or projects. Lessons feature short videos and exercises highlighting Google applications. Imagine doing the same, but with library resources rather than Google Apps. These lessons guide learners through the entire skill, highlighting the tools and tasks required at each step, scaffolding each video on the last. (Scaffolding is an educational technique in which students progressively move through a series of concepts and skills leading toward understanding and independence.) They are directly related to practical goals for all types of learners, with titles to match:

- Organize Group Projects in Google Sheets
- Write Using Online Research
- Track Your Monthly Expenses
- Update Your Resume for Your Civilian Job Search
- Prepare for FAFSA
- Make a Family Newsletter

Take for example the Applied Digital Skill *Negotiating Your Salary*, which guides the learner through a set of scaffolded microskills in 2–4 minute videos, such as: "List Details about Your Job," "Match Skills and Accomplishments to Employer Priorities," "Research to Compare Rates," and "Prepare for a Sensitive Conversation." The lesson ends with a Reflection exercise that measures the learner's self-efficacy in the skill and satisfaction with the lesson with a few short questions.

At the end of the lesson, Extensions are offered, which are related deep-dive lessons to expand your knowledge and skills. Upon completion, the user receives a Certificate of Completion. Learners can string lessons together to gain the skills required for Google Suite certification. A badging system would also work well with a program like this.

### *Aligning Instruction with the Course*

Align information literacy content and modules to course syllabus whenever possible, whether content is embedded in a course, contained in an online guide, or delivered via synchronous online information literacy sessions. Arranging content by week or assignment is ideal. If possible, work directly with the instructor, course coordinator, or instructional designer to integrate the library instruction into the learning objectives and ensure the instruction is scaffolding the right skills for success in the course. Occasionally, when instructors are not keen to collaborate, the librarian may need to create an online help guide with only the syllabus and/or most frequent student questions to indicate the most useful content and organization.

Even for on-site courses and programming, creating online instructional content that learners can access later, when they're actually doing the work, is necessary. The one-and-done instruction session is not sufficient. This may mean a website, LibGuide, or hashtag students can follow on Twitter to get librarian and peer help. Many K–12 and college classes that meet on-site also have an online component in an LMS where materials are shared, quizzes taken, or assignments uploaded. If you can embed library instruction or contact information there, it might get to students who would otherwise never go to the library site. You may even want to direct learners to a Google Drive or Dropbox location if you have significant content to share and no place to host it.

### A Note on Assessments

The current obsession with assessment in libraries and education can be burdensome. Of course, it is critical that we understand the impact our instruction has on learning outcomes and learner efficacy so that as educators we can iterate our approach, content, style, and delivery. I'm less convinced we need to assess every aspect of library instruction and service to assert our relevancy. Most importantly, learners need opportunities to take stock of their own understanding, retention, and ability to synthesize the information and concepts they're working with.

With this in mind, I believe the best approach to assessment in online instruction is to design an activity that results in a meaningful product you, the learner, and potentially peers can evaluate and to capture that evaluation, if possible. If the objective addresses creating and deploying a search strategy, have the student record themselves performing the search so that you or a peer can watch and provide feedback. For lessons on topic development, utilize a mind-mapping tool like Google Drawings and ask the learner to share it for others to learn from and make suggestions on. A more formative (and informative) online assessments can be done with online bibliographic tools such as Mendeley or Zotero, where citations and sources can be evaluated and commented on by librarians during and after literature review activities—and students walk away with a lasting bibliography.

If quizzes are your thing or you need quick quantitative data, building short four- or five-question review quizzes in the LMS or other online tool such as LibWizard covering key concepts, that learners can retake until they master the answers, are a simple and easy assessment method. If you have multiple modules in the course, one quiz per module, placed after the content and activities, is recommended. Use the LMS quiz tool if you or the instructor would like to capture the score or analytics within the LMS. If you are not using the LMS or the instructor prefers not to capture quiz grades or not to share grades with librarians, you may also consider using third-party embedded assessment/survey tools such as the free tool ProProfs to capture some assessment data. These don't have to be embedded in the LMS; they can be accessed through any browser as an embedded widget or through a

URL. If possible, ensure users get their scores and feedback on wrong answers immediately, so they can adjust their understanding while still engaged in the learning activity.

## Activities Should Be Grounded in the Learners' Own Experience or Personal Interest

When engaging learners in library, information, or media literacy instruction, embedding lessons into activities they are already interested in, already engaged in, or that they find meaningful will improve participation and retention. Take this possible flipped lesson on evaluating sources (see Table 6.2).

An activity such as this provides the learner autonomy in the selection of topic while grounding it in an experience and process they are familiar with and that is relevant to them. It's advisable to design lessons so that the examples can be easily swapped out while the instructional content itself can be reused with different populations. You may swap out YouTube tutorials with news sites, websites, or other online resources while utilizing the same structure and tools. Whatever the example is, participants should be able to easily relate it to their own experience or interests.

When planning out discussions or activities, encourage students to share why they chose a particular topic, video, or resource along with personal reflections on their learning. Learners that have grown up with social media expect to share experiences and opinions with their online peers. Try not to limit responses and interactions to text. A mix of textual communication as well as animations, videos, GIFs, or multimedia presentations will expand their digital tool wheelhouse and keep Millennial and Gen Z learners engaged. If you're flipping your information literacy session, try starting the postactivity discussion online via the LMS or social media to get a temperature of the engagement level before your synchronous meeting. As part of self-reflection, consider encouraging a learner or group who could not complete the assignment or who had difficulty doing so, to share with the group. Ask other students or groups to assist. This type of interaction builds community and feeds younger learners' needs for recognition.

## Develop Technology-Enriched Activities That Are Interactive or Collaborative, with Possible Individual Pathways to Completion

At the core of this approach is the philosophy that instruction and meaning in the classroom should be designed in conversation with the learner. We are guides on the side, or even "meddlers in the middle," not sages on the stage (Judd and Marcum, 2017, 136). Active learning emphasizes learner involvement in doing, thinking, and connecting, and it's not that large of a leap to include them in the design of the activity as well. And according to

**Table 6.2  Sample Lesson on Source Selection and Evaluation**

| |
|---|
| **Lesson: Source Selection and Evaluation Using YouTube Video**<br>**Level: Introductory**<br>**Modality: Online, Flipped** |
| **Objectives:**<br><br>• Students will identify features of a source that can be used to determine credibility, relevancy, and currency.<br>• Students will think critically about how to apply criteria to an online source. |
| **Duration:** ~30 minutes<br><br>**Discussion:** Small group, entire class<br><br>**Tools:** YouTube; Google Slides or PowerPoint |
| **Setup:**<br><br>Ask the student to select a YouTube tutorial video that they would use in their own life. It may be about gaming, makeup application, DIY, becoming a YouTuber, or any topic they choose. Ask them to create a short presentation using Google Slides or PowerPoint. It should include a screen grab of the video homepage and the following information: |
| **Prompts:**<br><br>• How did you search for this video? What words did you use? What filters did you use, if any?<br>• How did you decide to watch this video? What are the qualities of the thumbnail, title, and description that indicated it will be useful for you? List at least three.<br>• For the videos you did not click on, why did you not select those? What are the qualities of the thumbnail, title, and description that indicated they would not be useful for you? List at least three.<br>• What in your experience led you to make those decisions? |
| **Discussion:**<br><br>As the students share their experiences, ask them to reflect on these questions and encourage them to note that while they may not have been actively thinking of this selection criteria, they were likely applying criteria. Bring into the discussion credibility and selection bias.<br><br>Lead discussion into how criteria can be applied to other content they need and how criteria differs based on what the content is used for. Makeup tutorials are selected with different criteria than gaming tutorials, but there is some crossover, such as number of hits, number of videos the creator has already made, and number of followers they have. Does that popularity imply their content is more accurate? Do we prefer newer tutorial or older ones? |

*(continued)*

**Table 6.2**   (*continued*)

| **Application:** |
| --- |
| Connect the discussion to evaluating online research resources. What kinds of criteria might be applied to news stories, books, or scholarly articles? What are the indicators we scan for in titles, abstracts, and dates that could help us select the best resources while making sure we get a balanced understanding of the topic? |

our understanding of learner characteristics, many of our learners would appreciate self-directing their learning or would benefit from gaining experience in doing so. There is evidence that adapting a diverse set of technologies to learning activities increases engagement in online learning (Desilets et al., 2017, 206).

Chapter 3 introduced tools and lessons promoting interactivity and community building in the virtual classroom using social media, citation tools, and LMS discussion boards. Here, I'd like to explore tools that students interact with individually or collaboratively that support them in building multimedia, interactive content for themselves and their fellow learners to share in. Providing an array of tools for them to choose from; allowing them autonomy in their topic or subject; and supporting them in choosing to work in groups, pairs, or singly are all ways to empower self-direction as you deploy these digital tools in your instruction. The incorporation of technology into the interactivity or collaboration is imperative to fully building the skill set these learners need. The capacity to navigate the digital sphere and create meaningful, well-cited, communicative content is as important as any information literacy lesson laid out by ALA or its subcommittees.

### *Collaboratively Annotate a Video*

From the University of Minnesota, VideoAnt is a web-based tool that allows groups to collaboratively annotate YouTube videos. Videos may be posted by the instructor, already available on YouTube (think news broadcasts, political ads, TED talks) or posted by a student. The group annotation function allows students to post, read others' comments, and reply to them, creating a layered, cumulative response from the group critiquing or analyzing a piece of media. The instructor may choose to insert reflective questions or their own annotations beforehand or during the students' interaction. This multimedia approach to analysis and communication taps into active learning methods, community-building needs, and learning preferences such as multitasking and connectivity.

### Building Interactive Stories with StorylineSJ, StorymapJS, and TimelineJS

Three excellent free tools from the Knight Lab, StorylineJS, StorymapJS, and TimelineJS help users create interactive line charts, maps, and timelines to visualize concepts such as population changes, historical events, biographies, gentrification, and landscape changes due to global warming. Students can work individually or in groups to create these mediascapes that bring together curated resources to tell stories and highlight primary sources. Activities utilizing these tools would certainly spark students' imagination while they learn to work with primary resources and archival or digital collections.

A recent librarian-designed project for TimelineJS asked students to gather images of their neighborhood (or a neighborhood they were interested in) from local history collections, social media, and websites. Students then correlated that with news reports from local papers and statistics from census resources to create a visual, historic timeline of their selected neighborhood. One of the most difficult steps in the process was researching the provenance of images to ensure they came from the right neighborhood—what a great lesson for the students to struggle with. The local nature of the topics and the connections participants felt with their own and other's neighborhoods forged tangible community ties within the learning group. (These are also great tools for building partnerships with faculty interested in assignments or projects around digital humanities, social sciences, and history.)

### Gaming (and Badging) Library Instruction

"Rather than learning through listening, games provide students with opportunities to engage through competition, participate in hands-on activities, and learn from mistakes."

—Margino, 2013, 334

Long a library staple to get students active in classrooms and at outreach events, digital games are a new way to activate even more students into learning about the library. Tools like Kahoot! help librarians create trivia or learning games that can be shared with the class and accessed via PIN by anyone with a browser. These can be played online or on-site, used for quick assessments, and lighten up the library instruction load for both librarian and learner.

Games also have the capacity to engender significant instructional design and learning theory, to become a powerhouse of instruction. Games put power into the hands of the players—they can choose to be competitive or just have fun, form an alliance or be a lone wolf, yell out the answer or follow along in their heads. And while they revel in their autonomy and gameplay, they're learning important literacy concepts, building skills, and engaging with library resources in a new way.

Upon realizing they were missing connection with about half of all students despite their robust information literacy program, librarians at Miami University in Ohio devised a Choose-Your-Own-Adventure game to teach information literacy concepts to the students they weren't reaching—and that they would increasingly miss due to decreasing library resources and personnel (Long, 2017). After consulting with faculty and librarians, they determined the game needed to be self-paced, simple, and meet core library concepts such as defining a topic, finding books, evaluating web resources, and citing sources. The text-based game was built in Twine, a linear storytelling platform, to mimic the feel of Choose-Your-Own-Adventure books. The group has plans to eventually upgrade the game to an RPG using Adventr, a platform supporting interactive videos.

For library orientations, Goosechase, a mobile app that helps you build scavenger hunts, is an interactive alternative that could be utilized by on-site student or online students, to familiarize themselves virtually with library spaces they may feel disconnected from. Student can post text, videos, or images as they work through the hunt to "prove" they found each answer.

Badging can tap into similar motivations as gaming. Badges are a kind of microcredential, used as evidence of proven skill, knowledge, or mastery, akin to achieving a certain level or rank in a game. Some recent studies have shown badging programs' positive impact on recognizing academic achievement and improving retention in higher education (Mah, 2016). School and university libraries have piloted digital badge programs, creating learning pathways wherein students gain badges for completing information literacy competencies aligned with various standards and frameworks. Badging programs for the use of specialized equipment in makerspaces or media labs are also popular—only once a patron earns a 3D printing badge are they allowed to schedule time on the machine.

Badging programs may rely on learners' intrinsic motivation to "collect" relevant badges for display on online profiles or on extrinsic motivation in which they are gathered for course credit or special privileges. If your campus or district has a badging initiative, make sure library and information literacy instruction is included as a set of earnable badges. The Chicago City of Learning program awards badges for extracurricular activities, including learning to make a video at the library. Alternatively, promote events or skills that help patrons earn badges from other organizations such as LinkedIn or NASA. Platforms such as WordPress, Credly, or an LMS are used to validate and display digital badges.

### *Visual Sharing and Dialogue*

Another way to get online learners sharing their stories, processes, feedback, or questions is by recording and posting them for you and others to view and reply to. In the age of selfies and TikTok many younger learners will be comfortable sharing themselves in video format. Steller.co is a free iOS and Android app that easily creates and shares visual stories. Alternatively, with a free account from Animaker or Powtoon students can create short animations just as easily and use them to express their thoughts, analysis, critique, or personal introduction.

For returning learners, emphasizing that learning digital tools improves their ability to incorporate technology into their jobs and lives; expands their digital skills set; and updates their knowledge regarding online resources will help ease the burden of learning these new tools, or at least justify it. Illustrate also how they will share this new skill set on résumés or LinkedIn profiles. Offering a variety of options to gain credit or achieve mastery of library skills and tying those skills to tangible outcomes will help alleviate the perceived burden.

## Reaching Out to Partners, Collaborators, Gatekeepers, and Innovators

Incorporating online library instruction into syllabi, course, and department learning outcomes, and into the LMS itself requires collaboration and partnerships across organizations. When identifying potential partners in instructional design and delivery, energetic individuals with skin in the game are a good place to start. Is there a new hire responsible for revamping an old course in need of information literacy instruction? Are there teachers in your district fired up about current topics, looking for resources, and helping to create lessons on current events? Is there a new chair or director responsible for developing online curriculum for a degree, certificate, or district effort? A faculty member eager to try a new online application or improve outcomes in a course? An instructional designer trying to implement accessibility methods? A power library user that considers themselves an expert in a certain online resource or application? These are all individuals who can help you build, promote, implement, and evaluate point-of-need and embedded instruction.

Although you want to work collaboratively and be adaptable, it is also wise to have some preset plans for what you want to build and achieve, along with a platform or two that can support it. It doesn't hurt to share proof you (or someone in the library) has expertise in this area by noting past projects and successes. Build all of this into a short proposal or elevator speech that can be shared whenever you run into someone that might be interested and that you're interested in working with. Emphasizing how your project will help relieve instructor burdens and contribute to learner success in a measurable way will further improve your chances of finding partners.

Eastern Kentucky University (EKU) Libraries implemented these strategies with much success. After a sustained campaign of outreach to campus faculty, administrators, academic technologists, IT personnel, and instruction designers, EKU Libraries are now included in the campus's online course design process. The library must be consulted whenever a faculty begins designing a new course—a requirement the library was able to get coded in distance faculty members' contracts. This led to almost 90 percent of EKU faculty incorporating library resources and services into their online course. The distance learning librarian has administrative access to the LMS, and librarians have been asked to sit on director level search committees for instructional development positions (Judd and Marcum, 2017, 139–141). This was after a long, deliberate campaign to find campus online instruction "gatekeepers" and partner with them.

At the University of North Carolina, Charlotte, a different but also very successful collaborative pathway was followed. Librarians and instructional designers at the university participated in a series of meetings where each group shared their goals and strategies for working with faculty in online courses. Although the goals were similar, described as "well-designed instruction with clear learning objectives and opportunities for assessment," the form differed, mainly in the librarians' focus on modules for information literacy versus the designers sixteen-week course-long approach to design (Tingelstad and McCullough, 2019, 616). However, using the ACRL *Framework for Information Literacy in Higher Education* and relevant readings including the book *Librarians and Instructional Designers: Collaboration and Innovation,* the group collaboratively designed six lessons around the frameworks' six frames, which includes concepts such as authority is constructed and contextual, information creation as a process, and research as inquiry. After these meetings a number of liaison librarians developed lasting collaborations with instructional designers that furthered the library's integration into the LMS, including the implementation of the LibGuides LTI tool and creation of a "librarian" role. Using their new understanding of what services and expertise the library offered, instructional designers increased their referrals of faculty to librarian partners and library spaces such as the library's Visualization Lab and EZ Video Studio.

Hot topics like news literacy can bring librarians, teachers, and instructional technology together, as well. Judy Bryson, the library media teacher at W. A. Carter High School in the Rialto Unified School District, was worried about how much exposure students in her region got to balanced, traditional news sources. She believed, "If students consume the news at all, it is often via social media or click baited headlines" (News Literacy Project, 2019). Bryson worked with online news evaluation resource Checkology and teachers in her school to develop news literacy programs that included badging and multimedia presentations.

Similarly, when teacher-librarian Jennifer LaGarde paired up with tech educator Darren Hudgins to travel across the country developing media literacy lessons for schools, they found instructors needed help building curriculum exploring the difference between digesting news on mobile devices versus larger-screened laptops or desktops. By working with teachers to find the best technology tools and news stories to highlight the visual limitation of reading news on Instagram apps, they improved the lessons and the potential impact on student learning (LaGarde and Hudgins, 2020).

## Conclusion

By applying established learning theories about user behaviors to our understanding of learner characteristics, we are able to develop informed approaches for building engaging, relevant, optimally located library, information, and media literacy instruction. The approaches include creating digestibly sized Digital Learning Objects (DLOs), ensuring the instruction is relevant to the learner and grounded in their own experience or interest, and intentionally introducing technology-enriched content to the activities and assessments to increase interactivity and engage the learning in knowledge construction. To do this successfully, we need to be not only open to new partnerships but seek them out in a thoughtful and sustained manner.

## References

Boling, Erica C., Mary Houg, Hindi Krinsky, Hafiz Saleem, and Maggie Stevens. 2012. "Cutting the Distance in Distance Education: Perspectives on What Promotes Positive, Online Learning Experiences." *The Internet and Higher Education* 15(2): 118–126.

Bowles-Terry, Melissa, Merinda Kaye Hensley, and Lisa Janicke Hinchliffe. 2010. "Best Practices for Online Video Tutorials in Academic Libraries." *Communications in Information Literacy* 4(1): 17–28.

Desilets, Michelle R., C. M. Larson, Michelle M. Filkins, and Jennifer DeJonghe. 2017. "Forging Connections in Digital Spaces: Teaching Information Literacy Skills through Engaging Online Activities." In *Distributed Learning,* eds. T. Maddison and M. Kumaran, 205–219. Oxford, UK: Chandos Publishing.

Detlor, Brian, Lorne Booker, Alexander Serenko, and Heidi Julien. 2012 "Student Perceptions of Information Literacy Instruction: The Importance of Active Learning." *Education for Information* 29(2): 147–161.

Georgas, Helen. 2014. "Google vs. the Library (Part II): Student Search Patterns and Behaviors When Using Google and a Federated Search Tool." *portal: Libraries and the Academy* 14(4): 503–532.

Howe, Neil, and William Strauss. 1992. *Generations: The History of America's Future, 1584 to 2069*. New York: HarperCollins.

Howe, Neil, and William Strauss. 2000. *Millennials Rising: The Next Great Generation*. Toronto: Random House.

Hussar, William J., and Tabitha M. Bailey. 2018. *Projections of Education Statistics to 2026 (NCES 2018–019)*. Washington, DC: National Center for Education Statistics, U.S. Department of Education.

Judd, Cindy, and Brad Marcum. 2017. "Developing Best Practices for Creating an Authentic Learning Experience in an Online Learning Environment: Lessons Learned." In *Distributed Learning*, eds. T. Maddison and M. Kumaran, 135–153. Oxford, UK: Chandos Publishing.

Kauffman, Heather. 2015. "A Review of Predictive Factors of Student Success in and Satisfaction with Online Learning." *Research in Learning Technology* 23.

Knowles, Malcolm. 1973. *The Adult Learner: A Neglected Species*. Houston: Gulf Publishing.

Knowles, Malcolm. 1984. *Andragogy in Action*. San Francisco: Jossey-Bass.

LaGarde, Jennifer, and Darren Hudgins. 2020. "It's Time to Go Mobile While Teaching News Literacy." *School Library Journal*. https://www.slj.com/?detailStory=teaching-news-literacy-jennifer-lagarde-darren-hudgins-fake-biased-news-reporting.

Lim, Doo H., and Hyunjoong Kim. 2003. "Motivation and Learner Characteristics Affecting Online Learning and Learning Application." *Journal of Educational Technology Systems* 31(4): 423–439.

Long, J. 2017. "Gaming Library Instruction: Using Interactive Play to Promote Research as a Process." In *Distributed Learning*, eds. T. Maddison and M. Kumaran, 385–401. Oxford, UK: Chandos Publishing.

Magnuson, Lauren. 2019. "Embracing Embeddedness with Learning Tools Interoperability (LTI)." *New Top Technologies Every Librarian Needs to Know: A LITA Guide*. Chicago: ALA Neal-Schuman.

Mah, D. K. 2016. "Learning Analytics and Digital Badges: Potential Impact on Student Retention in Higher Education." *Technology, Knowledge and Learning* 21(3), 285–305.

Manwaring, Kristine C., Ross Larsen, Charles R. Graham, Curtis R. Henrie, and Lisa R. Halverson. 2017. "Investigating Student Engagement in Blended Learning Settings Using Experience Sampling and Structural Equation Modeling." *Internet and Higher Education* 35, 21–33.

Margino, Megan. 2013. "Revitalizing Traditional Information Literacy Instruction: Exploring Games in Academic Libraries." *Public Services Quarterly* 9(4): 333–341.

Merriam, Sharan B., Rosemary S. Caffarella, and Lisa Baumgartner. 2007. *Learning in Adulthood: A Comprehensive Guide*, 3rd ed. Hoboken, NJ: John Wiley & Sons.

Mestre, Lori S. 2012. "Student Preference for Tutorial Design: A Usability Study." *Reference Services Review* 40(2): 258–276.

Mohr, Kathleen A. J., and Eric S. Mohr. 2017. "Understanding Generation Z Students to Promote a Contemporary Learning Environment." *Journal on Empowering Teaching Excellence* 1(1): 9.

Mune, Christina, Crystal Goldman, Silke Higgins, Laurel Eby, Emily K. Chan, and Linda Crotty. 2015. "Developing Adaptable Online Information Literacy Modules for a Learning Management System." *Journal of Library & Information Services in Distance Learning* 9(1–2): 101–118.

News Literacy Project. 2019. "On the Frontlines of News Literacy." *School Library Journal*. https://www.slj.com/?detailStory=on-the-frontlines-of-news-literacy.

Oh, Kyong Eun, and Mónica Colón-Aguirre. 2019. "A Comparative Study of Perceptions and Use of Google Scholar and Academic Library Discovery Systems." *College & Research Libraries* 80(6): 876–891.

Pigliapoco, Erika, and Alessandro Bogliolo. 2008. "The Effects of Psychological Sense of Community in Online and Face-to-Face Academic Courses." *International Journal of Emerging Technologies in Learning (iJET)* 3(4): 60–69.

Poole, Herbert. 1985. *Theories of the Middle Range.* Norwood, NJ: Ablex.

Robinson, Heather, Whitney Kilgore, and Scott J. Warren. 2017. "Care, Communication, Learner Support: Designing Meaningful Online Collaborative Learning." *Online Learning Journal* 21(4), 29–51.

Rovai, Alfred P. 2001. "Building Classroom Community at a Distance: A Case Study." *Educational Technology Research and Development* 49(4): 33–48.

Rush, Lucinda, and Rachel Stott. 2014. "Minute to Learn It: Integrating One-Minute Videos into Information Literacy Programming." *Internet Reference Services Quarterly* 19(3–4): 219–232.

Seemiller, Corey, and Meghan Grace. 2017. "Generation Z: Educating and Engaging the Next Generation of Students." *About Campus* 22(3): 21–26.

Swan, Karen. 2004. "Learning Online: Current Research on Issues of Interface, Teaching Presence and Learner Characteristics." In *Elements of Quality Online Education: Into the Mainstream,* eds. J. Bourne and J. C. Moore, 63–79. Needham, MA: Sloan Center for Online Education.

Taylor, Mark L. 2006. "Generation NeXt Comes to College: 2006 Updates and Emerging Issues." In *A Collection of Papers on Self-Study and Institutional Improvement,* Vol. 2, ed. Susan E. Van Kollenburg, 48–55. Chicago: Higher Learning Commission.

Tingelstad, Catherine, and Heather McCullough. 2019. "Instruction Librarians and Instructional Designers: A Natural Collaboration." *College & Research Libraries News* 80(11), 616.

Webb, Kathryn Kavanagh, and Jeanne K. Hoover. 2015. "Universal Design for Learning (UDL) in the Academic Library: A Methodology for Mapping Multiple Means of Representation in Library Tutorials." *College & Research Libraries* 76(4): 537–553.

Westmeyer, Paul. 1988. *Effective Teaching in Adult and Higher Education.* Springfield, IL: Charles Thomas.

Wilson, Michael, and Leslie E. Gerber. 2008. "How Generational Theory Can Improve Teaching: Strategies for Working with the Millennials." *Currents in Teaching and Learning* 1(1): 29–44.

Zipf, George K. 1949. *Human Behavior and the Principle of Least Effort: An Introduction to Human Ecology.* Cambridge, MA: Addison-Wesley.

# CHAPTER SEVEN

# Keep a Digital Toolbox: A Bibliography of Useful (and Mostly Free) Tools for Supporting Online Learning

## Introduction

This tool bibliography focuses on mobile apps, web-based applications, downloadable programs, and browser extensions that help librarians make engaging, interactive online content, promote peer learning and sharing, or support active learning activities. They are selected for ease of use, affordability (almost all are free or have free versions), and relevancy to increasing participation or interaction during online learning experiences be they synchronous or asynchronous, group or individual. Examples of applying these tools to instruction, reference, discussion, and peer learning activities can be found throughout this book.

## Tools

### Accessibility Tools

Below are a few of the most widely used tools in libraries for determining the accessibility of online learning materials. With all accessibility tools, make sure the ones you are using meet the most current standards set by federal, state, and local governments, along with the most recent version of Web Content Accessibility Guidelines (WCAG). Note that there are a number of paid tools that are highly relevant to librarians and educators that may be available from your organization but are not listed here due to cost.

### Amara

Amara Public is a crowd-source subtitling tool that allows anyone with an Amara account to add subtitles to public videos. This tool can be used by instructors to subtitle a video posted to YouTube or Vimeo or to assign students subtitling activities. (Freemium)

### ImTranslator

Browser extension for Chrome, Firefox, Opera, and Yandex, this tool translates entire webpages or selected text between over one hundred languages and provides natural-sounding text-to-speech in a wide variety of languages. Includes a dictionary function as well. Controllable entirely by keyboard. (Free)

### PAVE (PDF Accessibility Validation Engine)

Check your PDF documents for accessibility using this tool from Zurich University. PAVE will make most accessibility corrections automatically and suggest others for you to complete yourself. There is a 5-MB file size limit. (Free)

### WAVE (Web Accessibility Evaluation Tool)

WAVE offers a Chrome and Firefox browser extension that checks the accessibility of webpages you're creating or assigning. WAVE's website offers a real-time accessibility evaluation of any webpage just by pasting in the URL. Evaluation includes structural errors, contrast issues, and missing alt text. Highly recommended. (Free)

### WebAIM.org Contrast Checker

This simple, free website helps creators determine if their content meets the WCAG recommended color contrast ratio for optimal readability. (Free)

### YouTube Caption Editor

YouTube automatically captions most videos uploaded to its platform, with varying accuracy. The platform's Caption Editor can be used to improve these captions. (Free)

## Animation

Animating short lessons, announcements, and discussion posts may help make content more engaging and visually interesting. Asking learners to animate their discussion posts or responses builds digital literacy, increases engagement, provides relief from walls of discussion board text, and creates space for those anxious about their writing skills to communicate a little more naturally with their peers.

### *Animaker*

Create short animated videos to make your content pop. Easy drag-and-drop designing. Can make up to five 2-minute videos for free each month. (Freemium)

### *Plotagon*

Animate your message or lecture with custom avatars, locations, text and voice for more visual appeal and interest. iOS, Android, and Desktop versions. (Free, in-app purchases)

### *Powtoon*

Offers a large number of templates to animate lessons, messages, outreach material, etc. Easy-to-use, 100 MB of 3-minute videos can be made and exported at no cost. (Freemium)

## App Builders

Instructors may wish to build applications that deliver content, promote interaction, display schedules or events, or that offer quizzes and games for assessment and engagement. These tools should help with those efforts. Additionally, easy-to-use app builders can be integrated into assignments and activities for online learners. Students might create demos for potential businesses, develop apps promoting sustainability or social projects, develop knowledge-testing games, or mapping and wayfinding apps that explore places and times. The possibilities are truly limited only by your imagination (and time, of course).

### *Appmakr*

Provides tools to build free, easy websites optimized for mobile browsers. Low-coding, low-cost app developing and hosting options for iOS and Android also available. (Freemium)

### Appsbar

Offers users free app templates for building iOS, Android, and Windows applications. Large showcase of Appsbar apps will inspire you. (Free)

### Appypie

A popular no-coding-required free app builder that publishes directly to iOS and Android platforms. (Free)

### MIT App Inventor

Originally created by Google, this Android app creator has been helping educators and students quickly build apps with minimal coding knowledge since 2010. Now maintained by the Massachusetts Institute for Technology. (Free)

## Authoring

These are tools that support the creation and publication of webpages, blogs, slide sets, and web-based or PDF books useful for librarians working in online education settings.

### Adobe Spark

Adobe Spark creates webpages, graphics, and video stories using themes, icons, images, and templates available within the tool. Spark pages work on any size browser and offer endless scrolling for your site, story, portfolio, data visualization, or digital scholarship project. (Freemium)

### GitBook

An open source tool supporting the creation of open textbooks hosted in a GitHub repository. Great for creating and collaborating on coding and engineering books. (Free)

### Google Sites

Part of the Google App suite, Google Sites offers templates for most every type of website you need including course sites, project management, art portfolios, event promotion, and more. Unlimited collaborators can work on the site at no cost. (Free)

### Google Slides

Another product from the Google App suite, Google Slides provides free templates and most of the formatting options available from expensive slide-building software. Collaboration is easy and version review options makes changes simple to track. Download slide sets in a variety of formats, including PDF and PowerPoint, or share through a URL. (Free)

### PressBook

An eBook creation tool based on WordPress. Templates and themes make formatting easy, and front and back matter can be auto-generated. (Freemium)

### Prezi

Created in 2009, Prezi offers viewers a more dynamic, engaging experience than a traditional slide set as users move through a spatial journey of text, images, and video. Collaborative options exist, but presentations can be shared via URL only at the free tier. There is a learning curve to making Prezis, but it may be a nice change from making slides for every presentation. (Freemium)

### SlideShare

Although not an authoring tool itself, for over a decade educators have used slideshare.net to upload and share slide, infographic, document, or video presentations online. Originally a standalone product, in 2012 SlideShare was purchased by LinkedIn. User may rate, comment, and share content, as well as connect their presentations to their LinkedIn profiles. (Freemium)

### WordPress

One of the most popular and long-standing free blog and website builders, WordPress has an excellent user community, easy-to-use interface, and plenty of free templates. Developers build for WordPress so interoperability with your favorite third-party application is likely, and there's a plug-in for just about anything you want to do, including many dealing with accessible design. (Freemium)

## Bibliography and Bookmarking Tools

There are many citation tools available free on the Internet that help generate citations and bibliographies for researchers. Other programs help groups categorize and access bookmarks during individual or collaborate information seeking and research. The tools listed here are the more powerful, popular tools available for free that support individual and collaborative work.

### *Diigo*

A browser extension for Chrome and Firefox, Diigo is an established tool offering users the ability to bookmark, annotate, archive, and categorize web resources. Create groups within Diigo to share or build collaborative web resource bibliographies using tags for organization and discovery. (Free)

### *Mendeley*

A reference and research management software that can be used individually or collaboratively to build bibliographies and share research with a large network of users. Available as a web app, desktop application, mobile app, and browser extension. (Free, paid options for larger groups and more storage)

### *Zotero*

This reference and research management tool can also be used by groups to build and share collaborative bibliographies. Available as a downloaded desktop application that works in conjunction with browser extensions known as Zotero Connectors. (Free, paid options for additional storage)

## OER Repositories

Open Educational Resource (OER) repositories for reusable, openly licensed DLOs help educators find, construct, deliver, and share digital lessons, activities, and assessments using various media types. A number of universities host their own repositories, many in partnerships with nonprofit organizations and volunteers from the library and education community. Exhaustive lists of repositories and resources are available online.

### *Internet Archive (IA)*

A nonprofit digital library that offers free access to books, music, images, and other media that is outside of copyright or openly licensed. Most IA content is added through web-crawling, but users may upload and share their own content on the platform. IA content such as postcopyright and open access books can be added to your library catalog. IA also offers the Open Library, from which online users from any location may apply for a digital library card to borrow eBooks.

### MERLOT

This OER repository started by the California State University system allows educators to create and share multimedia DLOs with rich metadata making them discoverable and reusable. MERLOT also provides tools to create openly licensed web-based DLOs, modules or courses with html, text, embedded video, and images. Content may be submitted for peer review, and all users can rate and review OERs and modules.

### OERCommons

Developed by ISKME (Institute for the Study of Knowledge Management), OER Commons hosts OER from around the world. It offers Open Author, an authoring and remixing tool supporting the creation of accessible OER. A plug-in is available for quick publication between Github and the repository.

### Orange Grove

One of the earliest OER repositories, Orange Grove serves as Florida's statewide OER repository for educators, hosting openly licensed DLOs appropriate for all age levels. The repository can be integrated into an LMS, allowing users to search and use content within the learning environment.

## Digital Storytelling

An amazing way to engage students in information discovery, evaluation, and synthesis is to ask them to build a story. These online tools support activities that ask learners to seek out reliable, creditable information, supporting sources, and multimedia content they can present in a cohesive, interesting way for others to learn from and potentially peer review.

### Steller.co

Create visual stories using a free mobile app for iOS and Android. Use preset themes and in-app tools to create an engaging visual experience for others. Great for student video assignments. (Free, in-app purchases)

### Storyboarder

Available for Mac OS, Windows, or Linux, download this free program to your desktop to draw quick storyboards using a variety of in-program tools and options. Play your board to animate stories or processes. PDF, GIF, and other export and download options are available for sharing your Storyboarder projects. (Free)

### *StorymapJS*

This tool incorporates users' own slides and media with content from YouTube, Flicker, Wikipedia, SoundCloud, and more, to create story maps that take the viewer across space and time in an engaging visual journey. Developed by the Knight Lab at Northwestern University. (Free)

### *TimelineJS*

Also from Knight Lab, TimelineJS lets users create interactive timelines with their own videos, images, sound, and text or add content from the many media platforms available on the web. (Free)

## Interactivity and Flipping

Sharing video lectures, recorded whiteboard work, and textual content along with activities and questions that spur thinking or discussion makes for good instructional design. Asking students to complete these activities before on-site or synchronous meetings so that your time together is focused on interpersonal interaction and helping is good pedagogy. Some tools to help you with this:

### *Answer Pad*

Allows instructors to capture data and feedback from students using the web or iOS/Android app in real time during on-site or synchronous meetings. Adapt instructional content and style as you assess student learning on the fly. (Free)

### *TEDed*

Build interactive text reflections, short exercises, quizzes, and supporting resources around the YouTube video of your choice. Reuse ones already created or share yours on the TEDed platform. TEDed's simple interface is easy to use for those building or viewing the content. (Free)

### *VideoAnt*

From the University of Minnesota, this web-based tool offers instructors the ability to annotate YouTube videos with questions for analysis and short answer. It can also be used by students to collaboratively annotate videos with follow-up questions and comments, such as pointing out bias and critiquing arguments. (Free)

### VoiceThread

A popular tool with educators and especially librarians, VoiceThread offers the ability to turn PowerPoints, videos, images, and audio files into interactive content with exercises, quizzes, diagrams, and discussion opportunities. Can be used on all devices and embedded in the LMS. (Paid)

## Gaming and Badging

Games and badging have both proven to be effective learning tools. Gamification of information literacy content is well underway at many libraries with improved learning outcomes to show for it. Having students create games for each other that address library and literacy concepts can promote deeper learning and understanding, and help them formulate analytical connections between concepts and how they would be applied in real life. Badging has been implemented by many types of libraries to help learners level-up their literacy and technology skills. Here are a few tools proven to help with these efforts:

### Badge List

This platform supports OpenBadges, provides free lifetime hosting, and walks you through the process of designing your learning pathway. This includes choosing the right badges, testing them out on your team, and building individual badge portfolios for participants. Many libraries and educational organizations use Badge List for their programs. (Freemium)

### Badger

An Open Source badging platform that allows sharing and storing of OpenBadges. Badges can be shared on social media and be awarded through the LMS, an API, or using QR codes in the physical world. (Freemium)

### Buildbox Free

Build and export a 2D or 3D game for iOS or Android using the no-code-necessary Buildbox Free platform that you download to your local Mac or Windows computer. Offers a ten-part video tutorial on building games with art, sound, and music. (Freemium)

### Flippity.net

Create simple, free games in a variety of styles including Jeopardy!, word search, and scavenger hunts using Google spreadsheets. (Free)

### Flowlab.io

A tool to create up to three visually engaging online games for unlimited users. Games are created entirely in your browser; no coding skills required. Available for iOS, Android, and Windows. (Freemium)

### Goosechase

This tool helps you create digital scavenger hunts wherein students post videos, images, or text responses as they play the game on mobile devices. Available for iOS and Android, offers a variety of game templates. (Freemium)

### Kahoot!

This tool creates quick learning and trivia games to be shared with the entire class or learning community for testing knowledge and improving understanding. Kahoot! games are joined via a browser with a PIN provided by the game host. Can spark fun, social, synchronous learning opportunities. (Free for teachers and students)

### ProProfs Brain Games

A simple game maker for word searches, crossword puzzles, hangman, and word scramble. May be a fun way to get students making digital content that they can share with peers. (Free)

### Unity

A free game development platform, Unity is used by many educators and students to build immersive 2D, 3D, VR, and AR gaming environments across many operating systems. There is a learning curve and coding involved, but an active support community and wealth of training and help video make this a popular, well-loved tool. (Freemium)

### Wordables

A word cloud guessing game you create in an iOS app. Ask learners to determine the topic or keywords based on clues in a word cloud. (Free, in-app purchases)

## GIFs, Images, and Infographics

GIFs, images, and infographics are excellent ways to quickly display information for online users. These are also great formats to ask for as assignment deliverables. Many tools exist to make their creation and sharing easy—and to make them look good!

### Canva

A popular online tool for creating infographics, fliers, graphics for social media, and even résumés. Many templates, images, and icons are provided in the tool. Easy to use with lots of free content. (Freemium)

### EZGIF

Browser-based free GIF maker that provides instructions for new GIF makers; allows users to resize and optimize videos. (Free)

### FireShot

A Chrome and Firefox browser extension that takes screenshots of full webpages beyond the browser window confines. Copy/paste content or publish the screenshots as PDFs with working links, or as JPEG or PNG files. Some editing functions available from the extension. (Freemium)

### GIF MAKER *from* GIPHY

Available in your web browser or through iOS or Android apps, create free GIFs using the intuitive interface by uploading your own video or adding one through any video URL. Publish to share across platforms. (Free)

### GIPHY Cam

Also from GIPHY, this app records video from your mobile device as GIFs. Add filters and effects inside the app. Available for iOS and Android. (Free, in-app purchases)

### JuxtaposeJS

A simple tool that allows users to compare two images interactively. You just need two pieces of similar media to start, such as Google Earth photos of polar icecaps, historical landscapes, or a popular figure between two time periods. (Free)

### Piktochart

A web-based tool for infographics. You can use your own images or the many icons, clip art, and templates available inside the tool. (Freemium)

### Tagxedo

Offers a real-time word cloud generator that can be used during online conversations to understand trends or emphasis in discussions as they happen or as an asynchronous infographic tool. (Free)

### WordArt

A word cloud generator that allows you to customize shapes, fonts, and colors. (Free)

## Peer Review Activities

Peer review and grading exercises are valuable for both the reviewer and reviewee. They create opportunities for low-risk feedback and relationship building. A few free tools to facilitate this in an online setting:

### Flipgrid

Build better learning communities by having students create short video logs to share in the Flipgrid meeting space. They can also reply to others and in paid version have real-time discussions. Videos can be edited, and users may add whiteboard work, text, emojis, and links to their recordings. (Freemium)

### Peergrade

This platform allows peers to review each other's work anonymously using rubrics uploaded by their instructors. Many features are customizable, and the tool can be used for feedback on individual or group work. Feedback is tracked through a dashboard and can be flagged for instructor moderation. (Freemium)

## Podcasts and Sound Editing

Instructor podcasts are an interesting way to mix things up in regard to content delivery and could potentially take less time to create than videos. Asking students to make and share short podcasts or audio recordings is another active learning idea that could interest audible learners especially, who may not get as much stimulation as visual learners in an online environment. Some tools for audio creation, editing, and distribution:

### Anchor

Create, edit, host, and publish your podcasts using the iOS or Android platform with this free app. Will transcribe 1-minute sections of the podcast for sharing on social media. (Free)

### Ardour

Open Source digital audio tool for Mac OS and Linux that has some of the most popular features available in ProTools that support high-end recording, mixing, and editing. (Free)

### Audacity

Open Source multitrack sound recording and editing program that operates on Windows, Mac OS, and Linux. Completely operable by a keyboard, making it more accessible than most other editing programs. (Free)

### PodBean

Easy-to-use tool for creating, publishing, promoting, and getting analytics on a podcast. (Freemium)

### SoundCloud

This popular platform with over 175 million unique monthly users in around 200 countries can be used to host and share music and podcasts. (Freemium)

## Screencasting and Video Creation

On any given day, librarians create screencast tutorials on concepts and tools, record information literacy sessions, record our screens while answering reference questions, make videos for outreach, websites, and digital signage. Here are some recommended video and screen capturing tools to support those activities. Consider pairing with applications in the Interactivity/Flipping section to create active learning lessons.

### ActivePresenter

This application for Mac OS or Windows helps you create free, HD videos from your screen, your webcam, or any HDMI device. The tool offers editing options, text, and annotation capabilities. Videos can be exported in a wide variety of formats for free (with a watermark). You can also add quizzes and games. (Freemium)

### Animoto

Animoto allows you to create high-quality videos using easy drag-and-drop editing features. Use storyboard templates and add your own clips, photos, and titles to tell a story, share a lesson or emphasize topics within the video. (Freemium)

### HitFilm Express

Free video-editing software offering tons of VFX tools. Great for users who may not have access to the advanced tools available in Premier, Captivate, or Camtasia. (Free)

### Loom

A Chrome browser extension that works with Windows, OS, or iOS, Loom offers screen and webcam recording, editing, and sharing. Videos may be shared with a link or embedded HTML code. Free version allows unlimited recording time for up to twenty-five videos. (Freemium)

### Screencast-o-matic

A longtime favorite in libraries, this tool allows you to record your screen, zoom in for emphasis, or trim recording. Publish videos to their site or YouTube, and save files locally for publication and sharing. Advanced editing tools are available with paid versions. (Freemium)

## Surveys, Polls, and Quizzes

Librarians love surveys! We also love quizzes and interactive polls. These are great ways to engage students both synchronously and asynchronously. That huge quiz section on Buzzfeed is popular for a reason. Use these tools to enhance interaction, gather assessment information, and share what others are thinking with your online or on-site learners.

### Cram

Instructors or students can create free flashcard sets to share with others. Flashcard sets can be shared in and imported from Google Drive for collaborative creation. (Free)

### Poll Everywhere

Easy-to-use tool that creates feedback polls and surveys students can take real time using any device type. Results can be shared immediately through a URL or captured over time. Twenty-five maximum audience size with free version. (Freemium)

### Pollmaker

Create one-question sharable and embeddable polls perfect for social media or websites. Templates and customization available, as well as options for comments, setting times for the poll to open and close, and randomizing answer order. (Free)

### Socrative

Create exercises and games that engage students using smartphones, laptops, and tablets. Instructors can see the results of the activities and quizzes in real time and personalize lessons as they happen. (Freemium)

## Virtual/Augmented Reality and 360 Experiences

Virtual reality, augmented reality, and 360 experiences have long been of interest to the library community as a way of providing library orientations and wayfinding when a physical tour just isn't an option. Many AR/VR (Augmented Reality/Virtual Reality) and 360 experience builders are still experimental or in beta stages, but that just makes it more fun, right? Those recommended here are currently available with at least a small support community, but in this space doing your homework on platform sustainability is strongly recommended before building anything.

### GIPHY World

Add GIFs and stickers to the world around you and record to share. This iOS and Android mobile app creates an AR environment using GIFs. (Free, in-app purchases)

### Google Tour Builder

Create virtual tours using Google Earth locations by adding your own images and videos. Quickly order the locations and share with others. The Tour Builder gallery will inspire students and instructors to share their stories and place others' stories in geographical context. (Free)

### SceneVR

Take your 360, panoramic, or VR-ready photos and turn them into virtual navigable scenes. Can be embedded in website or an LMS. (Free)

### StorySpheres

Experimental tool that adds audio to 360-degree images for a multimedia storytelling experience. (Free)

### Thinglink

Make interactive images, video, or VR productions for 360 experiences and virtual tours. Free version offers tools to make static images in interactive digital learning objects. (Freemium)

## Web Conferencing

Many organizations have access to enterprise web-conferencing programs and may not need these free tools for synchronous meetings. However, not all do; and frequently, student groups and community members don't have access to those licensed products. For those that need free web-conferencing tools, consider the following:

### Google Hangouts

Hosting up to ten participants, Google Hangouts are well integrated into the Google Apps platform, meaning easy scheduling and inviting for those within the Google universe. Requires a plug-in to use, and there have been persistent issues with video quality through the life of this popular choice. (Free)

### Lifesize Go

This web-conferencing tool can host up to eight participants at once. Hosts invite participants through email or text. Participants can join from any devices' browser with no downloads or installations required. (Free)

### Skype

Downloading the full Skype app allows for ten participants to join in a single call using this granddaddy of free web-conferencing tools. Participants are added through individual user accounts, although integrations with Outlook and Office 365 make users in the Windows universe easy to add to Skype conversations. (Freemium)

### Zoom

Zoom Basic allows up to one hundred users to engage in an up to 40-minute call with screen sharing, breakout rooms, and local recording. Does require users to download an app to join the session, which they find via a URL. (Freemium)

## Whiteboarding and Brainstorming

Writing, drawing, mapping things out on a whiteboard—these activities have become somehow fundamental to many people's learning process. Doing these things together creates learning experiences that build group cohesion and help create learning communities. In virtual environments, you will need special tools to facilitate this type of interaction.

### Bubbl.us

Simple mind-mapping tool available in any browser that can be populated and exported as an image file without any account creation. Enhanced features including collaborative options available at paid levels. (Freemium)

### Coggle

Mind-mapping tool with an attractive and easy-to-use interface that can be used collaboratively. Download end products as PDFs or images to share with the free version. (Freemium)

### Padlet

Create a blank canvas for collaboration and brainstorming in this application that allows users to work together in small or large groups posting images or videos, commenting, and sharing documents and sound files. Share final Padlets on social media. Available in iOS, Android, or any web browser. Paid levels include Google Apps and LMS integrations. (Freemium)

### ShowMe

This iOS app turns your iPad into a recordable whiteboard. Create whiteboard lessons with unlimited recording time that can be shared or exported as MP4s. Students with the app can be grouped for collaborative whiteboard work. Excellent app for flipping classroom instruction. (Free, in-app purchases)

# Glossary

Throughout this work you will find terms and acronyms you may not be familiar with but that are frequently used in discussions or publications around online education and virtual library services. To help you navigate this new vocabulary, frequently used terms are provided here.

**Affiliated User**
Individual with short- or long-term official attachments to an organization. This attachment could be through a membership (such as a library card holder), enrollment, or employment.

**Asynchronous**
Events or communication not occurring at the same time. In online education, a course or lesson that does not require instructors or students to be online concurrently, or at the same time.

**CMS (Course or Content Management System)**
A Course Management System is a software platform that provides tools and an online environment for hosting digital content, frequently for online learning. Course Management Systems are considered more passive platforms than Learning Management Systems. CMS is also sometimes used for Content Management System, which is a software platform for building and delivering online content.

**Course Shell**
A course "site" in a Learning Management System (LMS). A course shell is often created for every course section and populated with content by instructors.

**Creative Commons License**
A public copyright license issued by the Creative Commons organization allowing authors and creators to give others permission to reuse, adapt, and share their work.

**Digital Divide**
A gap between people or regions that have ready access to technology and internet connectivity and those that do not.

### Discovery System

A system that searches a wide variety of databases and resources that have been preindexed to normalize metadata mapping, quickly delivering results to users based on relevancy algorithms. Users apply facets and filters in the discovery system interface to refine results.

### DLO (Digital Learning Object)

A discrete digital resource used to support a specific learning outcome or activity. Can be a lesson plan, quiz, video, etc.

### Federated Search

A federated search engine allows users to search multiple databases and resources in real time. Generally slower than discovery systems, and result ranking can be problematic due to metadata inconsistencies across resources.

### Freemium

A combination of the words "free" and "premium" indicating that a product or service has a tiered pricing model in which the basic service is free but additional features, content, and/or support are only available at some cost.

### F2F (Face-to-Face)

An interaction that takes place in-person, in a physical locality rather than a virtual one.

### ILS (Integrated Library System)

An enterprise library management system that integrates most core library functions such as cataloging, acquisitions, and circulation into a single platform.

### Learning Objective

Describes the instructor's goal or intention for the activity or course; the focus of the content of the course.

### Learning Outcome

The measurable outcome or product of the activity or course; the skill, competency, or knowledge the learner will take away from the activity.

### LibGuides

A Content Management System from the company SpringShare used by many libraries to create webpages highlighting information and instruction on specific topics, resources, majors, courses, or information literacy objectives.

### LMS (Learning Management System)

An enterprise software platform used for the delivery and management of online learning and assessment. LMS features usually include course and content management, assignment and quiz functions, automatic grading options and grade books, discussion boards, and a variety of third-party add-ons such as web-conferencing applications.

**Matriculated Student**
A student officially enrolled as a student at a college or university.

**Modality**
The particular mode in which something is experienced or expressed. Used here as the way in which the learner experiences the educational activity—online or in-person, synchronous or asynchronous.

**Nonaffiliated User**
A user that is not officially affiliated with or attached to an organization but that may be accessing the organization's resources.

**Nonmatriculated Student**
A student that is not officially registered or enrolled in a college degree program but that may be attending a course for credit.

**OA (Open Access)**
Resource for which there is unrestricted access (usually online), with no cost barriers. Usually refers to research output or scholarly materials such as data sets, journal articles, or manuscripts.

**OER (Open Educational Resources)**
Educational resources (digital learning objects, lesson plan, quizzes, courseware, etc.) that are freely available for reuse, adaptation, and sharing.

**Open Source**
Software for which the source code is freely available online for reuse, adaption, and sharing.

**P2P (Peer-to-Peer)**
Interaction between two individuals that are at or near the same level of learning or knowledge.

**Returning Student/Reentry Student**
A student who has returned to school or online learning after taking a significant break from education. Sometimes used as a synonym for adult student or adult leaner, as returning students are frequently older than their traditionally aged counterparts.

**Scaffolding/Scaffolded**
A teaching method that enables students to build skills and knowledge gradually in order to eventually achieve the learning goal autonomously, without instructor assistance.

**Self-Efficacy**
A person's belief in their own ability or capacity to complete a specific task or succeed in a given scenario.

**Semantic Search**
A search utilizing technique that seeks out meaning using ontologies and relationships rather than a search that seeks only literal matches of the keyword.

**Synchronous**
Events or communication that occur at the same time, here used to indicate a course or lesson during which instructor and students are working concurrently, at the same time, or at the same pace.

**Web-Scale Discovery**
Products or services that index a wide variety of physical collections, print and electric journals, and online resources to make them keyword searchable through a single search box.

## About the Author

**Christina D. Mune,** MLIS, was the online learning librarian for San Jose State University in San Jose, California, before serving as the director of information technology services and most recently as associate dean of innovation and resource management. After supporting one of the first higher education MOOC trials between San Jose State and Udacity, she has been exploring how libraries can contribute to student success in all types of online learning environments. This exploration has led to numerous publications and presentations on the academic library's support of online learning, digital literacy, and the adoption of open educational resources. With *Libraries Supporting Online Learning: Practical Strategies and Best Practices*, Mune shares her full kit of technology tools, pedagogical strategies, and tested methods for all practitioners seeking to up their online librarianship game.